Born in London in 1939, Alan Ayckbourn spent most of his childhood in Sussex and was educated at Haileybury. Leaving there one Friday at the age of seventeen, he went into the theatre the following Monday and has been working in it ever since as, variously, a stage manager, sound technician, lighting technician, scene painter, prop-maker, actor, writer and director. These talents developed thanks to his mentor, Stephen Joseph, whom he first met in 1958 upon joining the newly formed Library Theatre in Scarborough. He was a BBC Radio Drama Producer from 1965 to 1970, returning to Scarborough to take up the post of Artistic Director of the Theatre in the Round, left vacant after Stephen Joseph's death in 1967. Since that time, he has premièred over thirty of his plays, first at the Library Theatre and, from 1976 onwards, at the company's new converted base, the Stephen Joseph Theatre. Over twenty of his plays have subsequently been produced either in the West End or at the National Theatre. They have been translated into thirty-two languages and have been performed in virtually every continent of the globe, receiving many national and international awards in the process.

INVISIBLE FRIENDS

ALAN AYCKBOURN

ff

faber and faber

LONDON · BOSTON

First published in 1991
by Faber and Faber Limited
3 Queen Square London WC1N 3AU

Photoset by Parker Typesetting Service Leicester
Printed in Great Britain by
Cox & Wyman Ltd Reading Berkshire

© Haydonning Ltd, 1991

All rights whatsoever in this play are strictly reserved and applications for
permission to perform it, etc., must be made in advance, before rehearsals begin,
to Margaret Ramsay Ltd, 14a Goodwin's Court, St Martin's Lane,
London WC2N 4LL

A CIP record for this book is available from the British Library

ISBN 0-571-14476-4

2 4 6 8 10 9 7 5 3

CHARACTERS

LUCY BAINES
GARY, her real brother
JOY, her real mother
WALT, her real father
ZARA, her invisible friend
CHUCK, Zara's invisible brother
FELIX, Zara's invisible father

Scene: The Baines home.
Real and imaginary.

Invisible Friends was first performed at the Stephen Joseph Theatre in the Round, Scarborough, on 22 November 1989. The cast was as follows:

LUCY BAINES	Emma Chambers
JOY	Doreen Andrew
WALT	Bill Moody
GARY	Ian Dunn
ZARA	Jennifer Wiltsie
FELIX	Robin Bowerman
CHUCK	Sean Chapman
Director	Alan Ayckbourn
Design	Juliet Nichols/Geof Keys
Lighting	Jackie Staines

ACT I

*The Baines house. 5.00 p.m. Visible are a ground-floor living area,
and the kitchen leading off that. Stairs up lead to a corridor with
bedrooms leading off it. The visible rooms are Lucy's room, small and
tidy. She is that exception to the rule, a young teenage girl with an
excessive love of orderliness. Besides the bed, it has a small desk/work
table, an easy chair and a wardrobe/cupboard. A notice board filled
with her private lists and favourite sayings and quotations.*
*Next to hers is her older brother Gary's room. By complete contrast this
room is a tip. Clothes strewn everywhere, an unmade bed, cluttered
tables and chairs. Prominent among all the clutter is Gary's pride and
joy, his hi-fi equipment. At the start,* GARY *is lying on his bed atop a
mound of clutter that he hasn't bothered to move, listening to something
loud and aggressive. Something, fortunately, that we're unable, as of
now, to hear.* GARY, *in appearance, almost exactly matches his
room.*
Downstairs in the living area, drab and also rather untidy. WALT,
*Gary's and Lucy's father, lies slumped fast asleep in an armchair,
facing the TV which has on an early-evening news programme. We
can't, at present, hear this either. Looking at* WALT, *we can
understand who* GARY *takes after. Overweight and unkempt,* WALT
asleep is almost as unprepossessing as WALT *awake.*
In the kitchen, JOY, *wife and mother, is preparing tea. She does this,
as she does everything in life, with a great sense of sorrow. Seldom can
anyone have been more unsuitably named. She sighs to herself as she
moves about the kitchen. We hear none of this though, for we are as yet
still outside the house.* LUCY *now appears from along the street,
carrying her school bag. She stops as she reaches her house. Faint
traffic and perhaps a little urban birdsong.*

LUCY: (*To the audience*) It all started the Friday I came home from
    school to tell my family some exciting news. By the way, my
    name's Lucy Baines. That's my mother there in the kitchen.
    And my father pretending he's watching the telly but
    actually he's fast asleep. And that one upstairs, that's my

older brother – known usually as Grisly Gary. Anyway, you'll meet them soon enough because unfortunately they all feature in this story I'm going to tell you. As soon as you have met them, you're immediately going to wish you hadn't met them. I mean, they're all right. I suppose. Sometimes. Very, very, very occasionally. Like every fifth Christmas in June, they're all right. It's not that they're cruel to me or anything. I think they actually do love me, really, though you'd never know it most of the time. They're just so – gloomy and glum. Like you know that saying: 'Eat, Drink and Be Merry for Tomorrow We Die'? Well, my Dad's version of that is, 'Tomorrow We Die, So What Are You Looking So Cheerful About?' I mean, I don't expect them to leap about laughing all day long but, well, on a day like this for instance, when I came home on this particular Friday with this terrific news – it would have been nice to have had a really warm welcome.

(*She goes through the front door.*)

(*Calling as she goes*) Mum! Mum!

JOY: (*Immensely cheerily*) Lucy, you're home at last! How lovely to see you!

LUCY: Hallo, Mum.

(*They embrace.*)

JOY: Oh, you're looking so bonny. Have you had a good day at school? Tell me all about it.

LUCY: Wonderful, I've had a wonderful day. I have to tell you, Mum, it's so exciting – I've been chosen for the school swimming team.

JOY: (*With a cry of delight*) You haven't!

LUCY: I have! The relay and the 200 metres backstroke.

JOY: Backstroke! Oh, that's just wonderful. We must tell your Dad. Dad!

LUCY: Oh, don't wake him up . . .

JOY: No, I must. He'll want to know. Walt! Walter!

WALT: (*Waking up cheerfully*) What's that? What's all this?

JOY: Dad, listen to this, listen to this news . . .

WALT: (*Playfully*) Did I doze off? I must have dozed off.

JOY: (*Affectionately*) Yes, you did, you know you did, you old devil. And now you're awake you can just listen to Lucy's news.

2

WALT: News? What news is this? Come on, out with it, young Lucy.

JOY: Tell him your news.

LUCY: I will when you'll let me get a word in. Dad, I've been picked for the school swimming team . . .

(WALT *stares at her, speechless*.)

(*Shrugging modestly*) That's all.

WALT: The school swimming team?

LUCY: Yes.

JOY: Backstroke and relay.

WALT: (*Rather overcome*) Backstroke and relay?

LUCY: Yes.

(WALT *moves to* LUCY *and hugs her fiercely. He is obviously deeply moved.*)

WALT: I'm so proud, girl. I'm so proud of you. This is the proudest day of my life.

JOY: And mine, Dad. And mine.

WALT: Where's that lad Gary, then? We must tell Gary.

JOY: Oh, yes. We must tell Gary. (*Calling*) Gary!

WALT: (*Calling*) Gary!

(GARY, *at the sound of their voices, springs off his bed and starts downstairs eagerly.*)

LUCY: Oh, don't disturb him.

JOY: No, he'll want to know . . .

WALT: The lad'll want to know . . .

JOY: (*Calling*) Gary!

WALT: (*Calling*) Gary!

GARY: (*Having come downstairs*) Yes? What is it? (*Overjoyed*) Hallo, Lucy! Are you home from school already?

LUCY: Hi, Gary.

GARY: Did somebody call? What can I do for you?

JOY: Tell him your news, then.

WALT: Tell him your news.

LUCY: I've been picked for the school swimming team.

JOY: Two hundred metres backstroke . . .

WALT: And the relay.

(*A fractional pause, then* GARY *steps forward, picks up* LUCY *and whirls her in his arms.*)

3

GARY: (*As he does this*) YIPPEEE!
   (*A huge crowd starts cheering.*)
JOY: Hooray!
WALT: Bravo!
   (*The briefest burst of vigorous brass-band music. Before
   festivities can get under way, LUCY disengages herself from the
   riotous group and steps back outside the house again. Under the
   next, the others quietly resume their original starting positions.*)
LUCY: (*As she moves*) I mean, I didn't expect them to behave quite
   like that. But, you know, they could have at least said 'good'
   or something. 'Well done', even. But anyway, on this
   particular day, I came home from school – this is my house
   by the way – Number 162 Sycamore Street – it's just past the
   traffic lights and before you get to the zebra crossing, I don't
   know if you know Sycamore Street at all but – (*Breaking off
   again*) Sorry, I'm rambling again. On this Friday I came
   home full of excitement, with my fantastic news about the
   school swimming team.
   (*As LUCY enters the house, the traffic sounds disappear and are
   replaced by the noises inside. The TV drones on throughout and
   upstairs, faintly, the thud of Gary's music.*)
   Mum!
JOY: (*Without stopping her tasks*) Shh! Your father's asleep.
LUCY: (*Whispering*) Sorry! Mum, guess what?
JOY: Your dad's had a terrible day. His van broke down again,
   miles from nowhere . . .
LUCY: I've got this amazing news . . .
JOY: . . . he had to walk five miles . . .
LUCY: . . . go on, guess what happened to me today.
JOY: . . . by the time he'd phoned the AA and then walked five
   miles all the way back again, someone had stolen his front
   wheels . . .
LUCY: Shall I tell you?
JOY: Left his van standing on six bricks. I mean, I don't know
   what the world's coming to, I really don't.
LUCY: I'll tell you, shall I?
JOY: Stealing people's front wheels. I mean, what if your dad had
   been a pensioner? What if he'd been disabled . . . ?

4

LUCY: I've been picked for the school swimming team.

JOY: They should bring in stricter laws and stop all this vandalism in one fell swoop. I mean, the way we're going at the moment, none of us will be able to sleep securely in our beds . . .

LUCY: Two hundred metres backstroke. And the relay.

JOY: I mean, look at old Mrs Hadron. Those lads rode their bike right through her back garden. Ruined her bird table, cut up her lawn . . .

LUCY: Isn't that great news?

JOY: I mean, they should have been locked up. She's got no husband and her little dog's poorly . . . You see, if this council worried less about putting up new bandstands and building multi-storey car parks and a little more on making the streets safe from vandals and layabouts . . .

(LUCY *holds a conversation with herself.*)

LUCY: (*Under this last*) 'Tremendous news, Lucy. Absolutely fantastic. You're brilliant, I don't know how you do it . . .' 'Oh, it was nothing, Mum, really . . .'

JOY: (*Stopping as she sees* LUCY) What are you going on about there?

LUCY: Nothing.

JOY: What were you saying?

LUCY: Nothing. Just talking to myself, Mum. (*Under her breath*) As usual.

JOY: (*Suspiciously*) You haven't got that friend of yours back, have you?

LUCY: What?

JOY: That – invisible friend of yours? I hope you're not starting all that again?

LUCY: No.

JOY: You know how that annoys your dad.

JOY: Yep.

(*She moves away.*)

JOY: Where're you going?

LUCY: Upstairs. Put my things away.

JOY: Well, come straight down again. It's nearly tea-time. You can give me a hand.

LUCY: Right.

JOY: I've been on my feet all day, I've not had a minute's break since I got up, it's all right for the rest of you . . .

(JOY's *stream of complaining drops to a low mutter as* LUCY *moves out of earshot. She moves to where* WALT *is sitting asleep in front of the TV. As she nears him the TV fades up a little.*)

TV VOICE: And finally . . . more sobering economic news as the pound slumped lower still against a basket of other currencies. On top of that, inflation, as we heard earlier, is also up and indications are, according to the latest forecasts, that it will rise still further over the next three months. Later on this evening, in *Newsnight*, we shall be showing a special programme in which seven European economic experts will be giving their verdict: Is Britain's Economy a Sinking Ship? That'll be on *Newsnight* at 10.30 tonight. But now it's time to go over to Bert Cod at the London Weather Centre for the latest picture.

(LUCY *watches this for all of two seconds and scowls.*)

LUCY: (*To audience*) Even the TV's depressing in our house. We're only allowed to watch the programmes he wants to watch. And they're all dead boring. This is my father. Who's the current *Guinness Book of Records* twenty-four-hour sleeping champion. (*Loudly*) Whey-hey, Dad!!

WALT: (*Snorting awake*) Whah!

LUCY: Sorry, Dad, did I wake you?

WALT: (*Drowsily*) Not just at the moment, love, I want to watch the news . . .

(*He falls asleep again.*)

LUCY: (*To audience*) That was the extremely rare glimpse of my father awake. Would that we'd had a camera team here to capture that moment. No, I don't want to be too mean about Mum and Dad, but really . . . I don't honestly know why they're still together, if you want the truth. These days they don't even seem to like each other . . . I mean, don't get me wrong, I don't want them to start getting all lovey-dovey and daft . . .

(WALT *springs up from his armchair and faces* JOY *with adoration all over his face. She does likewise. They sing a brief*

6

excerpt from The Beggar's Opera.)

WALT: (*Singing*) 'I would love thee ev'ry day . . .'

JOY: (*Singing*) 'Ev'ry night we'd kiss and play . . .'

WALT: (*Singing*) 'If with me you'd fondly stray . . .'

JOY *and* WALT:(*Together*) 'Over the hills and far away . . .'
    (*They swiftly resume their original positions again.*)

LUCY: I wouldn't want anything like that, for heaven's sake.
    Yuk!

JOY: (*Calling from the kitchen*) Lucy, are you coming to help me,
    or not?

LUCY: Yes, Mum.

TV VOICE: (*Under all this*) Well, as to the weather picture, I'm
    afraid it's another gloomy one tomorrow as far as most of the
    country's concerned.

LUCY: With heavy rain mostly situated over Number 162
    Sycamore Street . . .

TV VOICE: As you can see there from our radar chart, this large
    area of low pressure here continues to sit over most of
    northern Europe. And that, of course, is causing those
    outbreaks of thunder we've been experiencing in certain
    areas, together with that virtually non-stop sleet and heavy
    rain which has also been affecting most regions during today.
    Tonight, well, it's going to get a good deal colder over most
    of the country, particularly up here in the north-east.
    Widespread frost, especially inland, with temperatures
    getting down in one or two places to as low as minus two or
    even three centigrade in some sheltered areas. And that
    promises to be more or less the picture over most of the
    country during the next day or so . . .
    (*During this,* LUCY *starts upstairs. As she moves away from the
    TV the sound fades down. Simultaneously, the rock music from
    Gary's room gets a little louder.*)

LUCY: (*As she goes upstairs, to audience*) Come with me, if you will.
    Upstairs. If you listen very carefully you can just hear the
    distant sounds of the greater spotted Grisly Gary, my
    unbelievably talkative brother. Grisly Gary is doing a
    building course at the technical college, training to be a
    bucket.

(*She reaches the door of Gary's room. The music is louder now.*)
Here we go. I'll just have a quiet word with him. Cover your ears.

(LUCY *opens Gary's door. The heavy-metal music comes up to a deafening level.* LUCY, *when she speaks, is quite inaudible.* GARY, *lying on the bed with his eyes closed, fails to notice her at all.*)

(*Mouthing, swiftly*) Hallo, Grisly. It's your loving sister, Lucy. Just to tell you I've been picked for the school swimming team. Thought you'd like to know. Bye, Grisly.

(LUCY *closes the door again. The music goes down to a lower level.*)

I enjoyed that chat.

(*She opens the door of her own room and goes inside.*)

This is my room. No one's allowed in here, except me. I'm a very tidy sort of person. Which is a bit extraordinary in this house. I think I must be a freak. I actually like to know where I've put things. This is my bed. That's my desk. And up there on the shelf. Those are my special, most favourite books.

(*The music pounds through the wall.*)

Actually, one of the reasons I keep it tidy is because my very, very best friend, Zara, also likes things tidy. Oh yes, I ought to explain to you about Zara. You may have heard my mum talking about my invisible friend. Do you remember? Well, that's my invisible friend, Zara. (*Introducing her*) This is Zara. I want you to meet Zara. Zara, say hallo. That's it. Will you say hallo to Zara, my invisible friend? I invented Zara – oh, years ago – when I was seven or eight. Just for fun. I think I was ill at that time and wasn't allowed to play with any of my real friends, so I made up Zara. She's my special friend that no one can see except me. Of course, I can't really see her either. Not really. Although sometimes I . . . It's almost as if I could see her, sometimes. If I concentrate very hard it's like I can just glimpse her out of the corner of my eye. (*She is thoughtful for a second.*) Still. Anyway. I've kept Zara for years and years. Until they all started saying I was much too old for that sort of thing and

8

got worried and started talking about sending for a doctor. So then I didn't take her round with me quite so much after that. But she's still here. And when I feel really sad and depressed like I do today, then I sit and talk to Zara. Zara always understands. Zara always listens. She's special. Aren't you, Zara? (*She listens to Zara.*) What's that? Yes, I wish he'd turn his music down, too. I've asked him, haven't I? (*Mimicking* GARY) 'How can I hear it if I turn it down, I can't hear the bass then, can I?' I used to have pictures in here but every time he put a disc on they fell off the walls. (*Pause. The music continues.*)

I mean, don't get me wrong. We like loud music, don't we, Zara? We love loud music. Sometimes. (*Yelling*) BUT NOT ALL THE TIME.

(*Pause.*)

Why doesn't he ever listen to quiet music? Just once. Wouldn't that be nice?

(*The music changes to a delicate piece of Bach, just for a second.* GARY *sits up in an attitude of deep appreciation, eyes still closed. Then the music resumes as before and he lies back down again.*)

But if he did that, he wouldn't be Grisly Gary then, would he?

(*Pause.*)

Oh, Zara, did I tell you I've been picked for the school swimming team? Isn't that exciting? Yes. Thank you. I'm glad you're excited, too. Good.

(*Pause.*)

(*Shouting*) IF ANYONE IS INTERESTED AT ALL, I WAS PICKED FOR THE SCHOOL SWIMMING TEAM TODAY. WHAT ABOUT THAT, FOLKS?

(*She listens. No reply.*)

Great. Thanks for your support, everyone. (*Tearful*) They might at least . . . They could have at least . . . Oh, Zara . . . I know you're always here, but sometimes I get so . . . lonely . . .

(*She sits on her bed, sad, angry and frustrated. Downstairs,* JOY *has come to the foot of the stairs and now calls up to* LUCY.)

JOY: Lucy, I told you to come straight down, do you hear me?

LUCY: (*Calling*) Yes, Mum.

JOY: Well, hurry up, then. And tell your brother tea's nearly ready.

(*JOY goes back into the kitchen. LUCY comes to a sudden decision.*)

LUCY: All right, then. Come on, Zara. I don't care what they say. Today you're coming downstairs to tea. If they won't listen to me I'll invite someone who will listen. Come on, Zara, down to tea.

(*Leading Zara by the hand, LUCY goes first into Gary's room. A burst of loud music as she enters. GARY lies as before.*)

(*Yelling*) Gary! Tea-time! Gary!

(*GARY doesn't hear her.*)

Gary!

(*She picks up a spray can of shaving foam from among the junk and sprays him with it. GARY sits up, indignantly.*)

GARY: Oy!

LUCY: Tea-time.

GARY: (*Swinging off the bed*) I'll get you, you . . .

(*But LUCY, with a laugh, is out of the room before he can catch her, slamming the door behind her. She now leads Zara downstairs. GARY ruefully mops himself down and in a moment switches off his sound gear and puts on his Walkman. He then goes off to the bathroom.*)

LUCY: (*To audience, as she goes downstairs*) Once, Zara used to come everywhere with me. I never left her behind for a minute. She used to sit with me at school and she came on holiday one year. And we even had to pack her a special suitcase. Dad was wild.

(*As LUCY passes WALT, still asleep in his armchair, we hear a brief excerpt from a gardening programme. This fades as LUCY reaches the kitchen.*)

TV VOICE: . . . and there's a very wide species of these. Some of them are evergreen and some deciduous. So make sure you get the right sort. They've lovely bright flowers and fruits. Like this chap here. There, who can ask for anything more colourful? And the good thing about *Berberis* is that he's not too fussy about the soil . . .

LUCY: Here we are.

JOY: (*Suspiciously*) Here who are?

LUCY: Me.

JOY: At last. Where have you been? Never mind. You can lay the table, it's nearly ready.

LUCY: OK. (*To Zara, still holding her hand*) Come on then, Zara.

JOY: What?

LUCY: Nothing.

JOY: What's the matter with your hand?

LUCY: Nothing.

JOY: Have you hurt it?

LUCY: No.

JOY: Well, don't be so silly and lay the table.

LUCY: Yes, Mum.

(*During the next* LUCY *lays the table with five places and also brings up an extra chair.* JOY *doesn't notice, she is so busy preparing the meal.*)

JOY: (*As they do this*) I saw Mrs Hedges today in the street. She was just coming back from the doctor's. She's no better. And her Ted's legs are going. He can barely take his weight on them now. Only a matter of time. And her Arthur's hand's still useless. She doesn't know which way to turn, I can tell you. Not that she can turn at all, poor woman, not with her back the way it is.

LUCY: Mum . . .

JOY: She was in agony just talking to me. Tears of agony. She shouldn't have been out except she can't bear to stay in. Not now her Tom's gone.

LUCY: Mum . . .

JOY: And then I met Mrs Bracewell – don't interrupt me, I'm talking, Lucy – she's had a chapter of accidents, too. Just got over her poorly foot and then her son rings up to say he'd broken both his legs skiing. So I don't know who she's going to get to lift her Maureen out of bed . . .

LUCY: (*To audience*) As you see, conversation is very much a one-way business in this house . . .

JOY: . . . and all that on top of her dog going. I mean, I don't know how she keeps cheerful, I don't.

(*She pauses briefly.*)

LUCY: (*Seizing the opportunity*) Mum . . .

JOY: Oh, yes, and talking of that, old Mr Perkins, you remember him, he used to give you barley sugars, well, he's passed on at last. I saw his daughter, Mrs Clarke, with the hip, in the supermarket. She said it was a great relief to them all. Mind you, I don't know how Mrs Perkins will cope now without him. She's very feeble these days and all.

LUCY: Never mind, Mum. On the brighter side . . .

JOY: Have you called your brother?

LUCY: Yes. A really good thing happened to me today . . .

JOY: Call your father then. I can hear all that later.

LUCY: Right.

JOY: I'll hear it later.

(JOY *moves back to the kitchen.*)

LUCY: Yes. (*To herself*) I bet. (*To Zara*) Come on, then.

(*She crosses to* WALT *who is still asleep. As she does so, we hear more of the gardening programme.*)

TV VOICE: . . . the real question of course is how much to cut off. Well, if you look at any branch of a shrub, like this one here, you'll see that the tip is soft and green. Now if you look from there back towards the main stem, you'll see a ring marking the end of last year's growth – just there, you see? There's your old wood. And there's your new wood. Now, you want to cut back, almost to your old wood, just about – there. Like so. And that's where your new shoots will be. And that's where your flowers are going to grow. Now, that's your winter or early-spring varieties. There's nothing mysterious about pruning. All it takes is good old-fashioned common sense and a little tiny bit of know-how . . .

(*During the next,* GARY *comes downstairs with his Walkman on. He is in a world of his own. He goes to the table and sits nodding to the silent music.*)

LUCY: Dad! Dad! (*She shakes him.*) Tea-time.

WALT: (*Snorting awake*) Just a minute, love, I'm watching this.

LUCY: Tea's ready.

WALT: I'm watching this, love.

LUCY: (*To audience*) Why's he watching this? It's a gardening

programme and we haven't even got a garden.
(*They watch for a moment.*)

JOY: (*To* GARY) Will you be out tonight, Gary? (*Louder*) Gary?

GARY: (*Lifting one earphone*) What's that, Mum?

JOY: I'm saying, are you going out tonight?

GARY: Yes, I'll be out with Ronnie and Billy and Jimmy and Tel.

JOY: Oh, that'll be nice.

LUCY: (*To audience*) Ronnie and Billy and Jimmy and Tel are
Gary's special mates. From the tech. Also training to be
buckets. Except Tel, who's studying to be a pile of sand.

WALT: What's all this we're watching?

LUCY: I don't know. You had it on.

WALT: I don't want this. Who put this on?

LUCY: You did.

WALT: I wanted the film. I'm missing the film.
(WALT *jabs the remote control. TV changes to western music. A
little dialogue. A lot of gunshots.*)
That's better.

LUCY: (*To audience*) Oh no. Westerns. I hate westerns . . .
(JOY *brings a casserole dish to the table. A burst of country music.
The lights change.*)

JOY: Here y'are, boys. Y'eat this up while it's still good and hot,
y'hear?

GARY: Yahoo, Maw. Is that a clam bake ah spy theyur?

JOY: Nope. This'n just plain old bacon 'n' beans, boy. You get
them down inside you.

WALT: Better get your vittals, son. We got a long hard, dusty ride
tomorrow, boy . . .

GARY: Yippie! Yeah, Paw. Yee-haw!
(*The music stops. The lights revert to normal.*)

LUCY: No. I think I prefer things the way they are, really . . .
(JOY *brings the casserole dish to the table.*)

JOY: It's on the table.

WALT: (*Keeping his eyes glued on the TV set*) Right.
(WALT *sits at the end of the table, turned half away, watching
the TV.* GARY *sits jigging to his music.* LUCY *sits next to the
additional chair.* JOY *returns with four bowls. She starts to serve.*
LUCY *gets up and crosses to the kitchen cupboard.*)

13

JOY: Where are you going, Lucy? Sit still and have your tea.

LUCY: Just getting an extra plate, Mum.

JOY: I've got enough here.

LUCY: No, we've got – (*Indicating the extra place*) Look.

JOY: (*Realizing*) Oh, no.

LUCY: Zara's here.

JOY: Oh, no, she isn't.

LUCY: She is. Promise.

JOY: Well, I'm not serving extra food to her . . . I'm not going through all that again. She's not having any, I'm sorry.

LUCY: All right, she can have mine.

JOY: Lucy! I'm warning you.

LUCY: I'll share mine with her . . .

JOY: Walt! Walter . . .

WALT: Just a second, love. I'm just watching this.

JOY: Tell this girl. You tell her. I'm not having this again. I'm not going through all that. Double meals. Double loads of washing . . . Double baths . . . I'm not starting all this again . . .

WALT: (*To the TV*) Yeah!

JOY: Walter!

WALT: What's that? I'm sorry, love, what's the problem?

JOY: Tell this girl I'm not having that so-called friend of hers back here again.

WALT: Back where?

JOY: (*Indicating Zara's place*) There!

WALT: Friend? I can't see any friend.

JOY: No, her invisible friend. That one. That Sarah.

LUCY: Zara.

WALT: Oh, no. We're not having that, Lucy. We've had quite enough of her, thank you very much.

LUCY: Zara's got to eat . . .

WALT: Well, I'm sorry. Not at my table. You clear that place right away, do you hear me?

LUCY: Then she'll starve, won't she?

WALT: (*Sharply*) I said, clear it away. At once, Lucy!

JOY: There! That's your dad telling you that, do you hear?

(LUCY *gets up and starts to clear the place away to the kitchen.*)

14

LUCY: It'll be your fault if she dies of starvation.

WALT: Damn good job if she does. The sooner the better.

JOY: Oh now, Walter . . .

WALT: What?

JOY: You mustn't talk like that. Even about . . .

WALT: Even about what?

JOY: Well, even about invisible people. I don't think that's right. You mustn't wish them dead.

WALT: What are you talking about, she's not even alive.

JOY: Well, maybe she isn't alive, I don't know. But you still shouldn't wish her dead, it's not right.

(LUCY *returns to the table.*)

WALT: Rubbish. (*To* LUCY) And you can put that extra chair back as well.

LUCY: (*Indignantly*) You mean Zara has to *stand* all through the meal, as well?

WALT: (*Fiercely*) DO AS YOU'RE TOLD! You'll get no tea in a minute.

JOY: You hear that, Lucy? You'll get no tea.

LUCY: (*Muttering*) I don't want any tea.

WALT: You won't get any tea at this rate.

LUCY: I don't want any tea.

JOY: Now, now, that's enough of that, just come and eat your tea.

LUCY: I've said, I don't want any tea.

WALT: You do as your mother tells you, girl, and eat your tea.

JOY: You hear that, Lucy? That's your dad telling you that.

(LUCY *returns the extra chair.*)

I thought you'd grown out of all this, Lucy. (*To* WALT) I thought she'd grown out of it. I mean, most children grow out of it by this age. I mean, they do, don't they? How old is she now?

WALT: (*Back to the TV*) Just a minute, love. I just want to watch this . . .

(LUCY *rejoins the table. A silence.* JOY *serves them with stew.* GARY *suddenly drums vigorously on the table, in time to his tape.*)

GARY: Ter–rer . . . ter–rer–ter–rer . . .

JOY: Don't do that, Gary. Not at the table.

15

GARY: (*Loudly*) Great track, this one, Mum.

JOY: Yes.

GARY: (*Beating time*) Even you'd like it. Tung . . . tung . . . tung
. . . tung . . . tung . . .

(*They eat in silence.* WALT *eats, half turned away.*)

LUCY: (*After a pause, to audience*) Another exciting meal time with
the Baines family.

(*A burst of gunfire from the TV.*)

Be great, wouldn't it, if one of those gunmen on the TV shot
Grisly Gary.

(*A gunshot.* GARY *clutches his chest and falls off his chair.*)

No, I didn't mean that. Not really.

(GARY *gets up off the floor and resumes his seat, looking slightly
puzzled.*)

I mean, don't get me wrong, I'm not saying that our meals
should consist of endless, boring, meaningless small talk like
this . . .

(*The other three immediately turn to face one another and burst
into very animated, very loud simultaneous conversation.*)

JOY: (*Very smart*) . . . and I caught sight of this dress in the
window and I just had to dash in and buy it, that very
instant. I said to Walter, 'I don't care what the cost is. If
necessary, I'll mortgage my *soul* to have it.' It's just
divine . . .

WALT: (*Simultaneously, equally smart*) . . . and the thing about
these westerns is, of course, that they're basically morality
tales. The age-old battle between good and evil, that's what
they boil down to . . . Which is what I find so absolutely
fascinating about them . . .

GARY: (*Simultaneously, equally smart*) . . . I mean, yes, I know, I
know, this sort of music is only a basic essential outlet for
youthful aggression. But look at it this way. Better
aggression channelled thus than through expressions of
violent, anti-social, much more public actions, surely . . . ?

(LUCY *cuts them off dead with a gesture. The meal continues as
normal.*)

LUCY: (*To audience*) . . . I'm not saying they should carry on like
that. Not at all. But it would be nice to have a *little*

conversation. If only, 'Pass the salt, please.' Is it any wonder I have to invent invisible friends? Can you blame me?
(*She turns to Zara, apparently standing beside her.*)
(*Whispering*) You all right just standing there, are you, Zara?
JOY: (*Looking up from her meal*) What's that, dear?
LUCY: Nothing. (*Whispering again*) Come on. Come and sit here with me. There's plenty of room.
(*She slides to the edge of her chair to make room for Zara.*)
That's better . . .
JOY: What are you doing now, Lucy?
LUCY: Nothing.
JOY: Well, sit properly. And eat your tea.
WALT: (*Watching the TV*) Whey-hey. He's marvellous, this one.
LUCY: (*To Zara, whispering*) Are you hungry, Zara? Would you like some of mine? Would you?
(LUCY *holds out a forkload of food to Zara's imaginary mouth, somewhere near her shoulder. Neither* WALT *nor* JOY *notices her doing this.* GARY *though, looking up momentarily from his plate, does. He stares at* LUCY *in amazement.*)
(*Unaware* GARY *is watching her*) Come on then, Zara, come on. Open wide, that's it. One big mouthful, that's it. Open wide.
GARY: (*Loudly*) What's she doing?
(LUCY *hastily stops and swallows the food herself.*)
JOY: (*Looking up*) What?
WALT: (*Looking round*) What's who doing?
GARY: Her. She was sticking her food in her ear.
JOY: What were you doing, Lucy?
WALT: Were you sticking your food in your ear?
LUCY: No.
GARY: Yes, she was. I saw her.
LUCY: I wasn't.
WALT: What were you doing?
LUCY: Nothing.
WALT: (*Fiercely*) What were you doing, girl?
LUCY: I was . . . (*Muttering*) I was – just giving some food to Zara.
GARY: To who? Who's she talking about?
WALT: Right. That's it. That's enough of that. I'm not having any

17

more of that. Upstairs. Do you hear me? Upstairs.

GARY: (*Rising*) I haven't finished my dinner yet . . .

WALT: Not you, you lunkhead. Her.

(GARY *sits again*.)

JOY: Oh now, Walter . . .

WALT: No arguments. UPSTAIRS!

LUCY: (*Leaving the table*) Right.

WALT: And you stay up there till you learn to behave yourself.

LUCY: Suits me.

WALT: And don't you argue with me, girl.

LUCY: I'm not arguing.

WALT: Oh yes, you are.

LUCY: I'm not, I'm agreeing.

WALT: (*Shouting*) What're you doing now if you're not arguing?

LUCY: (*Shouting back*) I'm agreeing.

WALT: Don't argue with me, you're arguing, girl. And don't walk away when I'm talking to you either. Come back here.

LUCY: (*Returning and sitting again*) Right. Make up your mind.

JOY: Now, now, now, now, now, now, now . . .

GARY: (*Rising*) What's everyone arguing about?

WALT: (*Savagely*) You, shut up!

GARY: (*Sitting*) Right.

WALT: (*To* LUCY) Upstairs!

GARY: (*Rising again*) Right.

WALT: Not you. Her.

GARY: (*Sitting*) Right.

LUCY: (*Rising*) Right.

WALT: And don't come down until you're ready to apologize, do you hear?

JOY: That's your father talking, Lucy. Are you listening to him?

LUCY: I can't help listening to him, can I, he's screaming at me. Come along, Zara. Say good night to everyone. Say good night to Zara . . .

WALT: UPSTAIRS!

(LUCY *starts upstairs*.)

Oh . . . oh . . . Sometimes, I could . . .

JOY: Now, Dad.

WALT: She can thank her lucky stars she's – she's who she is. (*To*

GARY) If she'd been you, lad, I'd have walloped her.

GARY: Eh? What's that, Dad?

WALT: Doesn't matter. Doesn't matter.

GARY: Can I have Lucy's tea, Mum?

JOY: You might as well, she's not going to eat it.

WALT: Give it him. Before he starts eating the table.

GARY: (*Grabbing her plate*) Ta!

JOY: He needs his food, Gary's a growing lad.

WALT: Well, I only hope his brain catches up with the rest of him, that's all.

GARY: What's that, Dad?

GARY: Eat your tea, genius.

(*Lights fade on the trio downstairs.* LUCY *is slowly entering her bedroom. She still holds Zara's hand. Under the next, they finish their tea downstairs.* JOY *quietly clears the table.* GARY *where he is, listening to his music.* WALT *watches TV.* LUCY *sits sadly on her bed.*)

LUCY: (*To audience*) So, I came upstairs again with Zara. Feeling even more depressed. Because I knew that, partly anyway, that had all been my fault. I knew what would happen if I brought Zara downstairs. I knew Dad would go mad. He always does. I think, in a funny way, they get like that about Zara because she frightens them. Well, the idea of her frightens them. Because they don't understand about her at all. But then people are always frightened of what they don't understand. They didn't understand why I needed her. Let's face it. They didn't understand, full stop. So I sat up in my room with no supper and I talked to Zara. Because she did understand.

(*Under the next,* WALT *and* JOY *come upstairs and go off to their bedroom.*)

And finally we stopped talking and Zara curled up on the end of my bed and fell asleep like she often did – and maybe I fell asleep, too, I don't know. And when I woke up I could hear Dad and Mum going up to their room to bed. And I thought about going in there and saying I was sorry to them both – and then I thought, 'No, why should I?' So instead, I switched off my light so they'd think I was asleep – (*She does this*.) Though I knew that really I should have gone and said sorry to them. That's what I should have done. Then none of what happened next would have happened. But it did.

(GARY *has started upstairs, too. He goes into the bathroom. Wind and rain sounds start under*.)

And then I heard it start to rain, and I went to the window, being careful not to disturb Zara, and I looked out – and it was a really dark night. The sort of night that makes you glad that you're safe and snug indoors. No stars, no moon, just the street lamps and this rain and wind lashing at the window. It looked like there was going to be a storm. And I was glad Zara was sleeping with me because – no, it doesn't matter.

(GARY *comes out of the bathroom in his pyjamas. Under the next he gets into bed under all the junk and goes to sleep*.)

And then I heard Gary coming to bed next door. And I hoped that tonight he wouldn't snore. Because when he snored it was almost as loud as his music. The walls in this house are made of old newspaper. And then I think I did sleep for just a few moments.

(*The house is now in darkness. Just a little street light on* LUCY *through her window, where she is sitting. She closes her eyes. A second's pause. Wind and rain rise. A clap of thunder.* LUCY *jolts awake*.)

It was the thunder that woke me. There was a terrible storm outside now and I suddenly felt rather frightened – and I turned to look for Zara but she wasn't on the bed any more. She'd gone. Zara had gone.

(*Lightning*.)

And now there was lightning . . .

(*Thunder*.)

And more thunder. And I went to turn on my light. (*She tries her light switch*.) Only it wasn't working. For some reason the lights weren't working. It must have been the storm. And I opened my door to go and see Mum and Dad . . . (*She does this*.) But as I did this, above the storm, I heard something – someone moving downstairs. And I thought at first it might have been Gary – he's always getting up in the night for a

sandwich – but I listened at his door –
(*She does so.* GARY *snores a little. Lightning.*)
And I heard him snoring.
(*Thunder.*)
It would take more than a storm to wake Gary.
(*A creak from the kitchen.*)
And I heard the sound again, coming from what sounded
like the kitchen. And I knew then it must be Zara. Zara was
down there. And I knew she wanted me. And I knew she
might be frightened, too. (*She gropes her way to the stairs.*)
And I felt my way to the stairs in the dark, trying not to wake
anyone. (*Calling softly*) Zara! Zara! Where are you? Zara! It's
me, Lucy. Don't be frightened. (*To audience*) And then it
happened. I was halfway down the stairs when –
(*Bright lightning and thunder in quick succession.*)
(*Over this, quickly*) There was this tremendous flash of
lightning and this huge clap of thunder and I must have
caught my foot on the stairs in the dark because the next
thing I knew I was falling . . . falling . . .
(LUCY *falls downstairs.*)
(*As she does so, with a cry*) ZARA!
(*She lands in a heap at the bottom of the stairs. Quick blackout.
Then quite soon the lights return, brightening as* LUCY *regains
consciousness.* ZARA, *a visible solid version now, stands looking
down at her.*)

ZARA: (*Concerned, her voice coming at first from a distance*) Lucy
. . . Lucy . . .
LUCY: (*Groggily*) Wah– wha– wha . . . ?
ZARA: (*Gently*) Lucy . . .
LUCY: Who're you . . . ? Who're you . . . ?
ZARA: Are you all right?
LUCY: Yes, I . . . Who are you . . . ? What are you . . . ?
ZARA: (*Helping her up*) Here. Come and sit down for a second.
(*She guides* LUCY *to the armchair.*)
You'll be all right. You just knocked your head when you
fell.
LUCY: (*As she sits*) Who are you? What are you doing in our
house?

ZARA: Don't you know?

LUCY: I've never seen you before in my life.

ZARA: Oh yes, you have, you know . . .

LUCY: You'd better tell me who you are at once or I'll call my parents . . .

ZARA: Can't you guess who I am, Lucy?

LUCY: I'll call my brother. Gary's very strong . . .

ZARA: No, he's not. Gary's a weed, Lucy.

LUCY: Don't say that . . .

ZARA: You said it yourself. You said it to me. 'Gary's a weed,' you said once . . .

LUCY: I've never even spoken to you –

ZARA: Lucy, you talk to me all the time. You tell me everything. Your deepest secrets. I know everything there is to know about you, Lucy.

LUCY: You can't. Nobody does.

ZARA: I know how you cried when Tracy Taylor said she wasn't going to be your friend any more because she said you'd cheated in French. Which you did. And you pretended you didn't care but afterwards you went and hid in the changing rooms on your own and you cried.

LUCY: I did not. That's a lie. . . .

ZARA: You did, I saw you . . . And the next day you brought some scissors to school that you took from the bathroom cabinet because you were going to cut up her French exercise book just to teach her . . .

LUCY: I did not. I never did that.

ZARA: No, not in the end, you didn't. But that was only because you got too scared to go through with it.

LUCY: How do you know all this? Nobody knows this.

ZARA: I do. Do you want me to tell you what happened at Peter Garforth's parents' house when you went to his birthday party?

LUCY: No . . .

ZARA: You wanted to use the toilet only it was busy so you went in his bath instead . . .

LUCY: (*With a wail*) I did not.

ZARA: I saw you, Lucy. I was there.

22

LUCY: You couldn't have been. Who are you? The only person who could possibly know that is . . . is . . .

ZARA: Yes.

LUCY: Zara. (*Incredulously*) Zara?

ZARA: Hallo, Lucy.

LUCY: Zara. You can't be Zara. She's invisible. You're invisible.

ZARA: I still am.

LUCY: But I can see you.

ZARA: Only you. Nobody else can. I'm still invisible to everyone else.

LUCY: Then how can I see you? What's happening?

ZARA: If you believe anything strongly enough, it can happen. You believed in me, Lucy. You believed in me so much that I'm here. I've come to stay with you.

LUCY: For ever?

ZARA: If that's what you'd like.

LUCY: Oh, yes. Oh, yes, yes, yes! Please.

ZARA: Then I'll stay.

LUCY: Oh, Zara . . .

(*She hugs her.*)

I've been so unhappy, you see. So lonely.

ZARA: I know.

LUCY: No one's interested in me – No one listens to me . . .

ZARA: I know. I know. It's all right. I'm here now. I'm with you, now. You must get some sleep. We'll talk again in the morning.

LUCY: Yes. OK.

(ZARA *helps* LUCY *to her feet. They start for the stairs.*)

Will you stay here tonight?

ZARA: I'll be here. Don't worry. I'll never be far away.

LUCY: I still can't believe it. I can touch you. You're real, aren't you?

ZARA: As real as you are.

LUCY: But how – ? I still don't see . . .

ZARA: I've told you. Believe in anything and it can happen. It's up to you. We don't ever use most of our brains. If we used them properly, we could see things, do things, go to places, make things happen that we've only dreamt about. You can do almost anything, if you put your mind to it . . .

LUCY: Anything?

ZARA: Almost.

LUCY: Like what?

ZARA: Well, you could do little things like this . . . Look. See the vase, on the table there. You could do this, for instance.

(*The vase moves several inches along the table, apparently of its own volition.*)

LUCY: (*Awed*) Gosh! Could I do that?

ZARA: With a little practice. Concentration. Just put your mind to it, that's all. Come on.

(*They go upstairs. During the next,* LUCY *goes into her room and lies on the bed.* ZARA *follows and stands in the bedroom doorway.*)

LUCY: (*To audience*) And at that moment, I felt the happiest I had ever been in my whole life. At last I had a real friend. At last I had someone to talk to. Someone who really understood. Someone who knew. The moment my head touched the pillow, I must have fallen asleep. I don't remember.

(*Yawning, drowsily*) I remember Zara standing in the doorway and I remember thinking . . . I must remember . . . thinking . . . to ask her in the morning . . . if . . . if . . . Mmmmm . . .

(*She falls asleep. The lights fade again. A second's blackout. Then they snap up again very bright.* ZARA *has gone.* JOY *is busy in the kitchen getting breakfast.* GARY *is still asleep. There is no sign of* WALT.)

(*Sitting up, abruptly*) And the next thing I knew it was morning. But I could no longer see Zara. Zara? Maybe I had dreamt it all. I don't know. Oh, please God I didn't dream it. Zara! But she was nowhere. And suddenly I was wide awake and I had to find her. I just had to find Zara.

(LUCY *leaps off the bed and runs out of her room.*)

(*Calling*) Zara! Zara!

(GARY, *in his bedroom, wakes up with a start.*)

GARY: (*Startled*) Wah! Whassat?

LUCY: (*Yelling*) Zara!

JOY: (*Calling from the kitchen*) What's that?

24

(LUCY *runs downstairs. Under the next* GARY *gets up and goes into the bathroom.*)

LUCY: Zara!

JOY: What on earth's the matter, Lucy? What are you shouting about, girl?

LUCY: (*Looking around, dismayed*) She's gone.

JOY: Who's gone?

LUCY: Zara.

JOY: Oh, now, I'm warning you – if you're starting that again –

LUCY: She was here. Zara was here, Mum, I saw her.

JOY: Now, you'd better stop this before your dad gets back, that's all. Because you know what'll happen if he hears you. He'll go completely off his trolley . . . Now, come and help me at once.

LUCY: (*Muttering*) She was here.

JOY: (*Sharply*) Lucy! That's your last warning. I'm not saying it again. (*Thrusting cutlery into* LUCY's *hand*) Lay the table and do as you're told.

(LUCY *reluctantly starts to do so.*)

LUCY: (*Muttering to herself*) I'll show her. I'll show them.
(*Her eye lights upon the vase on the table.*)
(*An idea*) Yes. What was it Zara said? You can do almost anything if you put your mind to it . . .
(*She stares at the vase and concentrates.*)
(*Frowning with effort*) Come on then. Move. Come on, move, won't you? Move!

JOY: (*Noticing her*) Lucy, what are you doing now?

LUCY: I'm trying to move the vase.

JOY: The vase?

LUCY: Yes.

JOY: I see. Well, I'll give you a little tip, shall I? If you want to move something you get hold of it, you see, like this, and then you wrap your fingers round it, like this, and then you lift it, like that, and then you move it to where you want to put it, like this, and then you put it down again, like that. It's a wonderful invention the human hand and God's been very generous and given you two of them, all right? Now get on with it. I think you're going barmy, girl. They'll lock you up for good one of these days.

25

LUCY: Very funny!

(*She starts to lay the table. After a second, having checked that* JOY *isn't looking, she tries again to move the vase.*)

(*Softly*) Come on!

(*Suddenly the vase moves very slightly but quite perceptibly.*)

(*With a cry*) I did it! I did it!

JOY: Did what?

LUCY: I moved it. I just moved the vase.

JOY: Did you? Well done. Now try putting the knives and forks down on the table. Practise doing that next, will you?

LUCY: Oh, Mum.

JOY: We're going to have to call the van out for you, I can see that.

(WALT *comes in through the front door. He has a newspaper with him.*)

WALT: (*As he enters*) Breakfast ready then, is it?

JOY: It will be. As soon as Flash Gordon here lays the table.

WALT: What's she doing now?

JOY: Moving the vase. That took her ten minutes.

WALT: Get a move on. Stop annoying your mother.

LUCY: Morning, Dad. Nice to see you, too.

WALT: That's enough of that. You're not too old, you know.

LUCY: Too old for what?

WALT: Too old for – for you know very well.

JOY: You know what he means. You listen to your dad.

LUCY: (*Muttering*) I don't know what he means . . .

(WALT *turns on the TV, sits in the armchair and reads the paper. In a moment, the sound comes up. A technical lecture.*)

TV VOICE: (*Under the next*) The phenomena associated with the flow of electricity in metallic conductors can be explained with the aid of the interaction of the elementary electric charge of the electron with the atoms of the metals. For convenience, the electrons are assumed to have a spherical shape. A metal very widely employed for the conduction of electricity is copper. It has a crystalline structure as we see here in this diagram. The nucleus of the copper atom contains twenty-nine positive elementary charges, which are neutralized by twenty-nine negatively charged electrons.

The twenty-ninth (outermost) electron is only very loosely connected to the atomic nucleus. Even at room temperature the thermal energy is great enough to enable the copper atoms to perform vibrations about their position of rest in the crystal lattice. As a result, these loosely connected electrons are, as it were, shaken off and thus become available as free carriers of negative electric charge for the conduction of electricity. These electrons are what we term 'quasi-free', that is they are repeatedly captured and released again. In the crystal lattice they behave rather like a gas in a container; for this reason the term 'electron gas' is sometimes employed as we see here. When a potential difference is applied between the ends of a conductor, electrons go from the negative to the positive pole. We see this illustrated here. The flow of electrons thus moves in the direction opposite to that of the current as conventionally defined . . .

(*The speech continues under until* ZARA *finally switches it off.*)

JOY: Come on, Lucy. Put these out as well.

(LUCY *fetches some more items and continues to lay the table for breakfast. While her back is turned,* ZARA *enters unexpectedly and sits at the table.* LUCY *turns and sees her.* ZARA *puts her finger to her lips.* LUCY *gasps and drops what she's carrying in surprise.*)

What are you doing now, girl? Pick them up at once.

WALT: Pick them up, you heard your mother.

JOY: Pick them up. Do as your dad tells you.

(LUCY *opens her mouth to argue, thinks better of it and picks the items up.*)

ZARA: (*Mimicking, as* LUCY *does so*) Clumsy!

LUCY: What – ?

JOY: What?

WALT: What?

LUCY: Nothing.

ZARA: Shh! Careful. They can't hear me, but they can hear you.

LUCY: (*Moving to the table, in a whisper*) Can they see you?

(JOY *at this moment brings something to put on the table.* ZARA *gets up and stands in front of* JOY, *waving her arms and calling.*)

ZARA: Yoo-hoo!

(JOY *doesn't react. She puts down what she is carrying and returns to the kitchen.*)
Apparently not.
LUCY: (*Whispering*) Where have you been, Zara? I thought you'd left.
ZARA: I was around. I told you. I'll always be around, somewhere. Don't worry. You'll never be alone again.
(GARY *comes out of the bathroom. He is now dressed. He starts downstairs. He has his Walkman on, as usual.*)
LUCY: (*Still whispering*) I moved the vase. Just now. I moved it with my mind.
ZARA: I know. I saw you. Well done.
(GARY *comes into the sitting room. He stops behind his father and reads the paper over his shoulder.*)
JOY: Ah, Gary, just in time. It's on the table.
(GARY *doesn't hear.*)
(*Louder*) Gary! Lucy, tell your brother his breakfast is ready.
(LUCY *crosses to* GARY *and lifts one earphone from his head.*)
LUCY: (*Bawling into* GARY's *ear*) YOUR BREAKFAST IS READY, GRISLY!
(GARY *and* WALT *both jump.*)
GARY: (*Alarmed*) What you doing?
WALT: Stop that! You stop that at once or you know what'll happen to you.
LUCY: No. What'll happen to me?
WALT: Never you mind. You know perfectly well what'll happen, I'm telling you.
JOY: There, Lucy. That's your father telling you what'll happen to you. It's on the table, Dad.
WALT: Right.
(WALT *gets up. He puts the paper down.* GARY *picks it up.* WALT *gets intrigued by what's on the TV screen.* GARY *takes the paper to the table and starts to read it as he goes. He is about to sit in the chair that* ZARA *is occupying.*)
LUCY: (*Softly, to* ZARA) Zara, look out.
(ZARA *swiftly rises from the chair.*)
ZARA: Whoops! Excuse me!
(*She bows as* GARY *goes to sit in the chair. She pulls it from*

28

under him at the last minute. GARY *sits on the floor.* LUCY *is amused.* ZARA *laughs.*)

GARY: Wah!

JOY: (*Alarmed*) Gary, are you all right?

GARY: (*Loudly*) I missed my chair.

JOY: Oh, dear.

WALT: (*To* LUCY, *suspiciously*) Was that anything to do with you?

LUCY: No.

WALT: You behave yourself.

GARY: I don't know how I missed my chair. I don't usually miss my chair.

(*They start to help themselves to cereal.* ZARA *hovers round the table watching them. The TV voice drones on.*)

JOY: Have you got the TV on for a reason, Walter?

WALT: No, I'm waiting for the boxing. Satellite.

(*None the less he seems fascinated with the current programme and gives little attention to the table, keeping his eyes glued to the TV screen.* GARY, *too, is absorbed in the newspaper.*)

JOY: Oh, that'll be nice. Cornflakes?

WALT: No, I'll have the Krispies.

JOY: (*To* LUCY) There you are. Pass your father the Krispies, Lucy. (*Shouting*) Do you want Krispies, Gary? Krispies?

GARY: No, I'll have Cornflakes, Mum.

JOY: Pass your brother the Cornflakes, Lucy.

(LUCY *does so. A pause. The adults are immersed,* JOY *in her food,* WALT *in the TV,* GARY *in the paper.* GARY *shakes a few Cornflakes into his bowl.* WALT *shakes a few Krispies into his. They pause just long enough for* ZARA *to give* LUCY *a smile and switch the bowls over.* WALT *is about to resume filling his bowl. He looks into it and stops.*)

WALT: Hang on.

JOY: What?

WALT: I've got Cornflakes here.

JOY: No, you haven't.

WALT: Yes, I have.

JOY: No, you've got Krispies. Those are Krispies. Look at the packet.

WALT: It may say Krispies on the packet. But they aren't.

(*Indicating bowl*) Look. These are Cornflakes.

JOY: That's odd. What's Gary got then?

WALT: (*Looking*) He's got Krispies.

JOY: He doesn't want Krispies. He wanted Cornflakes. He didn't want Krispies.

WALT: No, I'm the one who wanted Krispies.

JOY: That's odd. They must have put Krispies in a Cornflakes packet.

WALT: And Cornflakes in a Krispies packet.

JOY: Yes.

GARY: (*Waking up to the situation*) Hey. I got Krispies here.

WALT: Yes, we know. We know.

GARY: I wanted Cornflakes.

WALT: Yes, I know. Here, have these.

GARY: Ta.

WALT: Give me yours.

GARY: Right.

(*They exchange bowls.*)

WALT: Hey, you'd better give me your packet and all.

GARY: No, these are fine. I wanted Cornflakes.

WALT: I know you did. But those aren't Cornflakes, those are Krispies.

GARY: Are they? It says Cornflakes on the packet.

WALT: Yes, I know it says Cornflakes on the packet, but they're not Cornflakes, they're Krispies. Now give them to me. You can have these.

(*He gives* GARY *the Krispies packet and takes the Cornflakes from him.*)

GARY: I don't want these, I wanted Cornflakes.

WALT: Those are Cornflakes.

GARY: Are they? It says Krispies on the packet.

WALT: I know. But they're not Krispies, they're Cornflakes. The Cornflakes are in the Krispies packet and the Krispies are in the Cornflakes packet. Those are not Krispies, those are Cornflakes. And these are not Cornflakes, these are Krispies. Look.

(*He shakes some Cornflakes on to his Krispies.*)

GARY: Those are Cornflakes.

WALT: Cornflakes? How did they get in there?

GARY: It's a Cornflake packet.

(GARY *shakes some Krispies over his Cornflakes.*)

WALT: Those are Krispies, those are. How did they get in there?

GARY: In where?

WALT: In the Krispies packet? What the hell are the Krispies doing in the Krispies packet?

GARY: I don't know. Is that not right, then?

JOY: Can I help at all, Dad?

WALT: No, you can't.

JOY: Do you want me to scrape those Cornflakes off your Krispies?

WALT: No, I don't.

GARY: (*Offering the Krispies packet*) Do you want these back?

WALT: (*Angrily*) No, I don't. I don't want anything. I'll just have some toast. I'm going to write and complain about this.

JOY: (*To* LUCY) Pass your father the toast, Lucy.

LUCY: (*Doing so*) Dad?

WALT: (*To* LUCY) Was that anything to do with you?

LUCY: No.

(*She suppresses a giggle.*)

WALT: If I catch you smirking you'll go straight upstairs.

LUCY: (*Injured*) What have I done now?

WALT: You know, you know. You don't need to be told.

JOY: You know. You don't need telling.

(*The TV drones on.* GARY *carefully picks the Krispies off his Cornflakes and eats what remains.* ZARA *has wandered over and is idly sitting on the edge of the armchair, half watching the TV.*)

ZARA: This programme's extremely boring, isn't it?

LUCY: (*Unthinking*) Yes.

WALT: What?

JOY: What?

LUCY: Nothing.

WALT: Well, don't suddenly say 'yes' like that for no reason.

LUCY: No.

(WALT *looks at her suspiciously.*)

ZARA: Oh, I've had enough of this programme.

(ZARA *holds up her hand, cocks her thumb, lines it up, squinting*

at the screen, and operates it like a remote-control button. The
TV programme changes abruptly to some loud pop music.)

WALT: Oy!

JOY: What's happened?

WALT: The programme's changed. That's odd.

(*He locates the remote control. He returns the programme to what*
it was.)

That's better. That's better.

(ZARA *changes it back again.*)

(*Angrily*) What's going on here? Something's wrong with the
set now.

(WALT *changes it back again.* ZARA *changes again. They to and*
fro between channels for a bit.)

(*Wrestling with the control*) Damn thing . . .

ZARA: (*Finally losing patience*) Oh, I've had enough of this.

(*She gestures rather more emphatically at the screen. There is a*
loud bang from the TV set. A silence.)

JOY: Oh, goodness.

WALT: Now look what's happened.

GARY: (*Lifting one earphone*) What's happened?

JOY: The telly blew up.

GARY: (*Uninterested*) Oh.

WALT: (*To* LUCY) Have you been monkeying around with that
set?

LUCY: No.

WALT: I wouldn't put it past you. Well, that's that. I've missed
the boxing now, haven't I? Missed it.

ZARA: Well, it might be an idea if we all sat and talked to each
other, just for a change.

LUCY: Great.

WALT: What do you mean, 'great'?

JOY: Don't say that, Lucy. Your father's missed his programme.

ZARA: Good. Boxing's stupid, anyway.

LUCY: Extremely stupid.

JOY: Lucy!

WALT: Who are you calling extremely stupid?

ZARA: Two grown men battering each other senseless . . .

WALT: Who are you referring to?

32

ZARA: I ask you what would you rather do?

WALT: Lucy?

JOY: Lucy?

ZARA: Watch boxing or talk to me?

WALT: I'm asking you a question.

ZARA: Me or boxing?

WALT: Answer me! Who were you calling stupid?

ZARA: Boxing or me, Lucy?

WALT: Who?

LUCY: (*Confused*) You!

WALT: Right, that does it. Upstairs, this minute.

LUCY: What?

WALT: (*Yelling*) UPSTAIRS!

JOY: You heard your father.

LUCY: (*Rising*) I can't help hearing him.

WALT: You stay in your room till you're ready to apologize. I'm not having a daughter of mine calling me stupid under my own roof.

ZARA: Let's go out in the garden and call him stupid.

(LUCY *giggles despite herself.*)

WALT: And don't you start laughing, my girl, or you will be in trouble. Upstairs.

JOY: Upstairs . . .

LUCY: Dad, I didn't mean to –

WALT: (*Fiercely*) Upstairs.

ZARA: Come on, upstairs.

LUCY: Oh . . .

GARY: (*Looking up*) Where's she off to?

JOY: Upstairs.

GARY: Oh.

(LUCY *and* ZARA *go upstairs together.*)

LUCY: (*To audience*) At that moment, I was so angry – I was really so angry – I mean, it was just unfair. They blamed me for everything. Just everything. It was unfair. So I got angry, you see. I mean, that's the reason I agreed to . . . I didn't mean to hurt them, any of them . . . (*Lamely*) I just got angry, that's all.

(*She and* ZARA *are now in the bedroom.*)

33

(*To* ZARA) I hate them sometimes. I really hate them.

ZARA: Well. If you really hate them that much . . .

LUCY: What?

ZARA: Why don't you – get rid of them?

LUCY: Get rid of them?

ZARA: Why not? If you hate them?

LUCY: Get rid of them? How? You mean kill them?

ZARA: No, no. Nothing like that. Just make them invisible.

LUCY: Invisible? How?

ZARA: The same way you made me visible. The power of the
    mind, Lucy. Remember?

LUCY: I could do that? Really?

ZARA: Oh, yes. Easily.

LUCY: Just put my mind to it? Would it . . . ? Would it – hurt
    them?

ZARA: No. Not really. They wouldn't even know about it. They'd
    just disappear. That's all. No fuss. No mess. No questions.
    Just vanish like that. It's easy. Remember how you moved
    that vase? You did that. You just have to concentrate, that's
    all.

LUCY: That's all.

ZARA: Try it. Go on. Just close your eyes and concentrate.
    (LUCY *does so*.)
    Now try and picture them. Can you do that?

LUCY: Yes.

ZARA: Picture your father . . .

LUCY: Yes . . .

ZARA: Picture your mother . . .

LUCY: Yes . . .

ZARA: Picture your brother. Can you see them?

LUCY: Yes, I can see them.

ZARA: Right, now imagine them gone. Picture the empty
    table . . .

LUCY: Yes.

ZARA: Empty the picture. Can you do that?

LUCY: I'm trying. Can't you help me?

ZARA: No, you have to do it, Lucy. It has to be you. Come on,
    you can do it . . .

LUCY: Yes . . .

(*A strange eerie sound of a wailing, rushing wind, slowly approaching and gathering volume.*)

ZARA: That's it! It's working, Lucy, it's working. Come on . . .

LUCY: Yes . . .

ZARA: Make them go, Lucy . . .

LUCY: Yes . . .

ZARA: Make them vanish . . .

LUCY: Yes . . .

ZARA: Vanish!

LUCY: (*Loudly*) Vanish!

ZARA: (*Louder still*) Vanish!

LUCY: (*Still louder*) Vanish!

ZARA: (*Shouting*) Vanish!

LUCY: (*With a great scream over the furore*)

V–A–A–N–I–I–S–H–H!

(*Quick blackout. Silence. When the lights return the breakfast table downstairs is empty.* WALT, JOY *and* GARY *have all disappeared.*)

(*In a whisper*) Have they gone? Are they invisible?

ZARA: Go down and see for yourself.

(LUCY, *rather nervously, starts for the stairs. As she descends, frightened of what she might see, she calls out her family's names rather tentatively.* ZARA *follows her.*)

LUCY: (*Descending the stairs, calling*) Mum! . . . Dad! . . . Gary! Mum!

(*They enter the living area.*)

(*Looking at the empty table*) Mum . . . Dad . . .

(*A silence.*)

They've gone. They've really vanished. How long will they be gone for? How long?

ZARA: They'll be gone – till you really want them back. For ever if necessary.

(LUCY *moves to the table.*)

LUCY: (*A little nervously*) I may . . . I may want them back, sooner or later.

ZARA: That's up to you.

LUCY: I mean, even if I hate them – I'll probably miss them, too.

A bit. Fairly soon. I mean, I know you're here, Zara, but it
might still get a bit lonely. Mightn't it?

ZARA: (*Smiling*) Oh, no.

LUCY: No?

FELIX: Oh, no.

CHUCK: Oh, no.

(*As if from nowhere,* FELIX *and* CHUCK *have appeared. They
are a part of* ZARA's *'invisible' family and have, like her, a
pristine unreality about them. They stand smiling at* LUCY.)

LUCY: (*Startled*) Who are – ?

ZARA: Lucy, I want you to meet my family. This is my father,
Felix. And that's my brother, Chuck . . . Say hallo, Lucy.

LUCY: (*Weakly*) Hallo.

FELIX: Hallo, Lucy.

CHUCK: Hallo, Lucy. We've come to stay with you. Isn't that
nice?

FELIX: Isn't that nice?

ZARA: Isn't that nice?

LUCY: (*Weakly*) Lovely. (*To audience*) And how I came to live
with my new family – and how I got my own family back
again, I'll tell you in a little while.

(*She looks at the others, nervously.*)

(*To audience*) See you soon. Don't leave me for long, will
you?

(*Blackout.*)

ACT II

The same.
LUCY *comes on, looking very happy.*

LUCY: (*To audience*) Right. Let me tell you the rest of this story.
Are you ready? Well, the next few hours were the happiest in
my whole life. My real family had completely vanished – and
though at first I felt – well, a bit guilty – because I wouldn't
have wanted them to be hurt or anything – Zara told me that
they were perfectly OK. They weren't suffering or anything.
The way she explained it, they were just in another plane, like
in another universe, practically the same as the one we're in,
only running alongside it. But quite separate. It's difficult to
explain. Zara made it sound all very simple but then she's
brilliant sometimes.
(*During the next,* ZARA, *then* CHUCK *and* FELIX *come on. They
all sit at the table and start to play Snakes and Ladders.*)
Anyway, we all settled down to live happily together in the
house – Zara and me and Zara's brother Chuck who was just
great and her father Felix who was also very nice. We just
laughed and played games a lot and sometimes just talked. Or
rather I talked and they sat and listened. It seemed they really
wanted to hear what I had to say. Unlike some people I could
mention.

FELIX: Come on, Lucy, it's your go.

ZARA: Lucy, come on . . .

CHUCK: (*Resignedly*) She'll win again. She always does.

LUCY: (*To audience*) We played all sorts of stupid games, too. Like
Snakes and Ladders.
(LUCY *joins them at the table. She starts to shake the dice.*)

ZARA: Cheer up, Chuck. She can't win this time, she's miles
behind.

CHUCK: Bet you she does . . .

LUCY: (*To audience*) They weren't very good at games, though.
(*She throws.*)

37

(*To the others*) Six!

FELIX: Another go . . .

    (LUCY *moves her counter and makes to throw again.*)

ZARA: Get a one, go on get a one, then you'll go down the snake . . .

CHUCK: She won't get a one. She'll get a six.

    (LUCY *throws again.*)

LUCY: Six!

FELIX: Another six . . . !

CHUCK: (*Disgustedly*) I told you. I don't believe it.

ZARA: Well done! Another turn, Lucy.

    (LUCY *moves her counter and makes to throw for a third time.*)

CHUCK: Well, she can't get possibly get another six. Not possibly.

ZARA: Don't be too sure. Lucy's the champion, remember?

FELIX: Come on, champ.

    (LUCY *throws.*)

CHUCK: Oh, no . . .

LUCY, FELIX *and* ZARA: (*Together*) Six!

LUCY: I won! I won! I won!

CHUCK: Again! I don't believe it!

ZARA: Poor old Chuck. You must let him win sometimes, Lucy.

LUCY: (*Laughing and hugging* CHUCK) Sorry, I'm sorry, Chuck. Don't be angry with me, please don't be angry.

CHUCK: No, I'm not really. It's just that every game we play, you seem to win it.

FELIX: Well, I don't know about the rest of you but I think it's my bedtime. Chuck, you're the loser tonight. Loser tidies up, there you are . . .

    (FELIX *indicates the Snakes and Ladders.*)

CHUCK: Oh, not again!

ZARA: Loser tidies up!

LUCY: Loser tidies up!

CHUCK: All right! All right!

    (CHUCK *starts to clear the table.* FELIX *heads for the stairs.*)

FELIX: By the way, I saw in the paper tonight there was a funfair in town. I thought we might go to that tomorrow, if you'd like to.

ZARA: Oh, great . . .

CHUCK: You bet!

FELIX: Just a minute, just a second, you two. Does Lucy want to go, that's the point? It's up to Lucy, isn't it?

ZARA: Yes, sorry. Of course.

CHUCK: Sorry.

FELIX: Let's ask Lucy. Shall we go to the funfair, Lucy?

ZARA: Oh, say 'yes', Lucy.

CHUCK: Please say 'yes'.

LUCY: OK. We'll go to the funfair.

ZARA: Terrific!

CHUCK: Yes!

FELIX: All right. Funfair it is. Lucy has spoken. See you in the morning. I'll sleep in the front bedroom, if that's OK, Lucy?

LUCY: (*With a twinge of guilt*) Mum and Dad's bedroom. Yes, sure.

FELIX: Thank you. (*To* CHUCK *and* ZARA) And you two, remember to ask Lucy which rooms she wants you both to use. Remember it's her house and we're her guests and she's in charge. All right?

ZARA: Yes, of course.

CHUCK: Sure.

FELIX: Goodnight, then.

ZARA: Night!

LUCY: Night!

CHUCK: Goodnight.

(FELIX *goes up and off into Walt's and Joy's bedroom.*)

Well, where are you going to put me, Lucy?

LUCY: Well, there's my brother's room. Gary's room, I suppose.

CHUCK: Would that be OK?

LUCY: It's a bit untidy.

CHUCK: Oh, I'll soon tidy it up.

ZARA: Chuck's great at tidying.

LUCY: OK, I'll show you.

(*They start for the stairs.*)

It's next to mine. I think, Zara, you'll have to share with me . . .

ZARA: Sure . . .

(*As they go,* CHUCK *turns and, with a wave, switches off the downstairs lights.*)

LUCY: We've got a small folding bed. It isn't very comfortable, I'm afraid.

39

ZARA: That'll be fine.

CHUCK: Zara can sleep anywhere.

LUCY: That's my room and then here – this is Gary's room. You'll see what I mean by untidy.

(*She switches on the light and steps back to allow* CHUCK *to see the disarray.*)

CHUCK: Oh, dear. Yes, this is a big job.

LUCY: Shall we help you . . . ?

CHUCK: No, that's OK.

ZARA: Chuck will do it. He's good at tidying.

CHUCK: Just a second.

(CHUCK *frowns in concentration. The room 'tidies' itself. Objects shoot under the bed and back into cupboards. In the space of a few seconds, everything is clear.*)

LUCY: (*In disbelief*) Christmas!

CHUCK: That's better. Right. See you in the morning. Night. Sleep well.

ZARA: Night.

LUCY: (*Still dazed*) Night.

(CHUCK *closes the door and lies on the bed, eyes closed as if in meditation.*)

(*In a whisper to* ZARA) How did he do that?

ZARA: I've told you. If you want something enough, you can make it happen. All you need to do is put your mind to it.

LUCY: But it just tidied itself.

ZARA: No, Chuck tidied it. Chuck can do all sorts of things like that.

LUCY: Well . . . I'll find that bed for you, hang on.

ZARA: Wait, there's no need for that –

LUCY: What?

ZARA: We'll do what Chuck did just now.

LUCY: How do you mean?

ZARA: Come on. Just concentrate.

LUCY: Concentrate?

ZARA: (*Closing her eyes and frowning*) What do we want to do? We want the folding bed that's in the cupboard along the passage there, we want to unfold it and put it up in your bedroom. OK?

LUCY: Yes, but –

ZARA: Come on then. Concentrate on doing just that. Are you ready? Close your eyes . . .

(*They both close their eyes.*)

Both together. And . . . one . . . three . . .

(*A brief blackout. When the lights return there is an additional small bed in Lucy's room.*)

LUCY: Did anything happen?

ZARA: See for yourself.

(LUCY *cautiously opens her bedroom door.*)

LUCY: (*Seeing the extra bed*) Zara, it worked. The bed's in here. It worked. We did it.

ZARA: Of course we did. (*She sits on the bed.*) Oh, it's quite comfortable. This'll be fine.

(*She lies on her bed.* LUCY *does the same.*)

LUCY: What else can you do then? I mean, just with your mind?

ZARA: I've told you. Practically anything. The more practice you have the better. Chuck can do much more than me because he's older. And as for my father – well, Felix is brilliant.

LUCY: What else can Chuck do?

ZARA: Oh, masses. He drives cars with no petrol in. He always makes it snow at Christmas. He was awful at school. He once drained the school swimming pool and filled it up again with red ink.

LUCY: Did he get into trouble?

ZARA: You bet. The P.E. teacher was swimming in it at the time. He was stained bright pink for months.

(*They laugh.*)

LUCY: I'm glad you're here, Zara. I mean, really here, not just imaginary here.

ZARA: I'm glad, too. (*Yawning*) Oh, I'm tired. Go to the funfair tomorrow, eh?

LUCY: Yes.

ZARA: That'll be good. Want the light out?

LUCY: Yes. I'll –

(*She makes to get up.*)

ZARA: No, no . . . Not like that.

LUCY: No, of course.

(She closes her eyes and concentrates fiercely. Nothing happens.)

ZARA: No?

LUCY: I can't do it.

ZARA: You will in time, don't worry.

> *(She waves her hand. The bedroom light goes out. There is still light through the window.)*

You'll soon get the knack of it.

LUCY: I hope so.

> *(Pause.)*

Zara . . .

ZARA: Mmmm?

LUCY: If – if Chuck is so good at – making things happen – like doing things with cars and swimming pools and so on . . . well, how come he can't win at board games? Like when he shakes the dice – he only throws ones and twos – never fives or sixes. Why does that happen? He should be able to throw any number he wants, shouldn't he?

ZARA: *(Sleepily)* I don't know. You'd better ask Chuck.

LUCY: *(Half to herself)* It's odd, that. Very odd . . .

> *(She lies awake, puzzling. ZARA, apparently, is asleep. In the next room, CHUCK laughs softly to himself. LUCY doesn't hear him. The lights change and it is morning. LUCY is asleep. ZARA bounds off her bed and runs out of the door. She shakes LUCY as she passes.)*

ZARA: Wakey, wakey!

LUCY: *(Awaking with a jolt)* Oh!

> *(ZARA runs along the hall and downstairs. Simultaneously, CHUCK leaves his bedroom and follows her, under the next. They, in turn, are joined by FELIX. All three sit at the table downstairs and wait.)*

> *(To audience)* The following morning, everybody seemed to get up at dawn. Everyone but me, that was. It was about now that things started to go wrong – just very slightly at first and then worse and worse – until it all became a real nightmare. I got up and went downstairs. *(She does so, during the next.)* Actually, I felt a bit rough. I hadn't been able to get to sleep for ages. Probably because the house had been so quiet. I never thought I'd say this, but I think I actually missed the sound of Gary's snoring.

(*She reaches the sitting room. The others are all sitting at table. They look at her expectantly.*)

(*To the others*) Good morning.

FELIX, CHUCK and ZARA: (*In unison, cheerfully*) Good morning!

LUCY: What are you all doing?

FELIX: Are we glad to see you!

CHUCK: You bet.

ZARA: About time.

LUCY: Why?

FELIX: We were getting hungry.

CHUCK: Starving.

ZARA: What's for breakfast?

LUCY: Breakfast?

FELIX: Well, it's half-past six.

LUCY: (*Appalled*) Half-past six!

CHUCK: Six thirty-two, actually.

LUCY: In the morning?

ZARA: Six thirty-three now.

FELIX: Any chance of something to eat, Lucy? I don't want to rush
     you. It's just that we really are starving. Aren't we?

ZARA *and* CHUCK: (*Together*) We certainly are!

LUCY: Oh. Yes. Well, couldn't you have . . . ? I mean, why didn't
     you help yourselves? There's probably food there. Mum
     usually has – had . . . food in . . . If you – If you –

FELIX: Oh, no. We couldn't do that.

CHUCK: We couldn't help ourselves.

ZARA: That wouldn't be right.

FELIX: After all, we are guests.

CHUCK: We couldn't go barging around in someone else's kitchen,
     could we?

ZARA: That would be terribly rude.

LUCY: (*Uncertainly*) Yes. OK. I'll see what we – I mean, I'm not
     very good at cooking . . . What would you . . . ? Anything
     you'd like? Especially?

FELIX: Oh. Not really. Just a few eggs.

LUCY: Eggs. Right.

CHUCK: Bacon, perhaps?

LUCY: (*Starting to hunt*) Bacon, yes. I'll see if we . . .

43

ZARA: Sausages?

LUCY: Sausages, I'm not sure . . .

FELIX: Fried bread, possibly.

CHUCK: Grilled tomatoes.

LUCY: Tomatoes, yes.

ZARA: Mushrooms.

LUCY: Mushrooms.

FELIX: Any black pudding . . . ?

LUCY: Black pudding? No, I don't think we've . . .

CHUCK: Bit of fillet steak . . .

ZARA: Smoked haddock.

FELIX: Kippers.

CHUCK: Kidneys.

ZARA: Kedgeree . . .

FELIX: Caviare . . .

CHUCK: Smoked salmon . . .

ZARA: *Pain perdu* . . .

LUCY: (*Loudly*) Just a minute. Just a minute. We haven't got all this stuff. Caviare? We haven't got that. You'll just have to have what we've got here.

FELIX: Yes, of course, Lucy.

CHUCK: We'll have what you've got.

ZARA: Of course.

FELIX: What have you got?

LUCY: We've got . . . (*She looks in the fridge.*) We've got . . . one . . . two . . . three . . . four . . . five fish fingers.

CHUCK: Five fish fingers?

ZARA: Yuk!

FELIX: Nothing else?

LUCY: Er . . . Some deep-frozen sprouts.

CHUCK: Deep?

ZARA: Frozen?

FELIX: Sprouts?

CHUCK: For breakfast?

LUCY: (*Indignantly*) Well, I didn't know you'd want breakfast, did I? I mean, I don't do the shopping. My mother does the shopping. Only my mother . . . isn't here. (*Pathetically*) I don't do the shopping. How am I expected to know?

44

ZARA: It's all right. It's all right, Lucy. We'll help you, won't we?

FELIX: Oh yes.

CHUCK: You bet.

ZARA: We'll all go shopping with you this morning and show you what to buy. All right?

LUCY: Yes, OK.

ZARA: So you'll know in future. And by tomorrow, you'll have everything you need and you'll be able to cook us a really huge breakfast.

LUCY: Am I going to have to cook it every morning?

FELIX: Why? Is that a problem?

LUCY: Well . . . ?

CHUCK: Are you busy doing something else, then?

LUCY: Well . . . I have to go to school, you know.

ZARA: Not till later, surely?

LUCY: Well, at eight fifteen, I do.

FELIX: Oh, we'll have finished breakfast by then, won't we? We like to eat early. Six thirty at the latest.

LUCY: But I'll have to get up at five or something to cook it.

ZARA: I'll wake you. I'm always up by then.

LUCY: Then if you're up, why don't you cook it?

ZARA: It's not my house. I couldn't cook breakfast in someone else's house. It would be terribly rude. I mean, if you came to stay at our house we'd never expect you to cook.

LUCY: Where is your house?

ZARA: We haven't got one.

CHUCK: Come on. Enough of this chat. What are we going to eat?

FELIX: Well, I think we're going to have to forget breakfast, Chuck. We're going to have to wait for lunch.

CHUCK: Lunch? What's for lunch then?

ZARA: What have you got us for lunch, Lucy?

LUCY: Lunch? Nothing. I haven't got you anything.

FELIX: Nothing?

LUCY: Nothing. Five fish fingers and deep-frozen sprouts.

CHUCK: What again? Fish fingers and sprouts? Do you have that for every meal?

LUCY: No . . .

CHUCK: Doesn't it tend to get a bit boring?

LUCY: No, of course we don't. I'm just telling you, that's all we've got, that's all. That's all we've got in the house to eat.

CHUCK: Oh, lord.

FELIX: Oh, dear.

ZARA: Oh, heavens.

CHUCK: I must say this is very depressing.

FELIX: Awful.

ZARA: Dreadful.

(*They all sit very dejectedly.* LUCY *looks at them, alarmed.*)

LUCY: I'm sorry. Don't be sad. It wasn't my fault. Please. Don't be like that. We were having such a lovely time. Tell you what, would you like to play a game?

(*Pause. They look at her.*)

You'd like to play a game, wouldn't you?

FELIX: (*Suspiciously*) What sort of game?

LUCY: I don't know – Snakes and Ladders?

CHUCK: No. You always win at that.

LUCY: Ludo?

ZARA: No. It's too complicated.

LUCY: Happy Families?

FELIX: Hardly suitable at the moment, is it?

LUCY: I know. What about Snap? That's easy. Snap. Look, I've got some cards here. Let's all play Snap.

(LUCY *finds the cards.*)

CHUCK: How do you play this Snap?

LUCY: Oh, you must know Snap. It's the easiest game in the world. Look, I'll show you. We deal out all the cards like this – (*She does this as she speaks*) – only you mustn't look at them – and then we take it in turns to put one down in front of us from our own pile face upwards – and when you see two cards that are the same, you shout out snap. And the first person to call it out, wins and takes all the cards on the table. And the person with all the cards at the end wins.

CHUCK: Sounds very complicated.

LUCY: Look, I'll show you. We'll have a go. I'll put a card down first. (*She does so.*) Like that. Now you, Zara. You do the same.

ZARA: Right.

46

(ZARA *plays a card*.)

LUCY: Now, Felix. Your turn.

FELIX: Yes.

    (FELIX *plays a card*.)

LUCY: Now you, Chuck.

CHUCK: (*Playing a card*) Snap!

LUCY: No, it isn't. You have to have two cards the same, before you shout snap. If you shout out snap when you shouldn't the cards should really go in a pool.

CHUCK: In a pool?

LUCY: Yes.

CHUCK: Won't they get a bit damp?

LUCY: No, not a real pool . . . it's a . . . Oh, it doesn't matter. My turn.

    (*She plays another card*.)

ZARA: Now me?

LUCY: Yes.

    (ZARA *plays a card*.)

FELIX: And me.

    (FELIX *plays a card*.)

LUCY: And snap. There's two cards the same, you see?

FELIX: Oh, yes.

ZARA: Oh, yes.

CHUCK: Is there? Oh, yes, so there are.

LUCY: I win. So I take all these cards.

CHUCK: She's won again, what did I tell you?

LUCY: So now I start.

    (LUCY *plays a card*. ZARA *plays a card*. FELIX *plays a card*. CHUCK *plays a card*. LUCY *plays another card*. ZARA *plays another card*.)

    And snap!

FELIX: (*Belatedly*) Snap – oh, yes. Too late. Very good. Well done, Lucy. Good game this.

ZARA: Very good.

CHUCK: Yes, I'm getting the hang of it now.

LUCY: It's not that difficult.

FELIX: No. Tell you what. Shall we play with the cards the other way up? Would that be more fun?

ZARA: Oh, yes, let's.

LUCY: The other way up?

FELIX: Yes.

LUCY: How do you mean, the other way up?

ZARA: With the cards the other way up, you know.

LUCY: But then you won't be able to play.

CHUCK: Why not?

LUCY: Because you won't be able to see the cards. You can't play Snap if you can't see the cards.

ZARA: Why not?

LUCY: Because you won't know what they are.

FELIX: You can guess what they are though, can't you?

LUCY: Guess?

CHUCK: Yes.

LUCY: That's stupid.

CHUCK: No, it's not.

LUCY: It is. What's the point of that?

FELIX: Come on, Lucy. Let's try it. We can give it a try.

ZARA: Let's give it a try.

CHUCK: Give it a try.

LUCY: (*Muttering*) I don't see the point. It's completely and utterly stupid.

FELIX: We'll see. Your go, Lucy.

(LUCY *puts down a card, face down.* ZARA *does likewise. So does* FELIX. *So does* CHUCK.)

LUCY: This is stupid. You can't see them.

ZARA: Your go, Lucy.

(LUCY *plays a card.*)

FELIX: (*Knowingly*) Ah ha!

(ZARA *plays a card.*)

CHUCK: (*Thoughtfully*) Oh ho!

(FELIX *plays a card.*)

ZARA: (*Pensively*) Hee hee.

LUCY: (*Exasperatedly*) What are you all doing?

(CHUCK *plays a card.*)

FELIX, ZARA *and* CHUCK: (*Almost together*) Snap!

(*The family laughs.*)

CHUCK: Who was first? Was it you, Zara?

48

ZARA: No, it was Felix. Felix was first.

FELIX: Me, was it? Was it me first, Lucy?

LUCY: I've no idea. I don't know what you're all doing. How could you know it was snap?

ZARA: Because Chuck played the same as you did, Lucy. Those are the rules, aren't they?

LUCY: How do you know his card's the same as mine?

FELIX: Because it is.

CHUCK: It's obvious. Look.

    (CHUCK *turns over his card*.)

ZARA: Now look at your card.

    (LUCY *does so. Hers and Chuck's are the same*.)

    You see?

LUCY: How did you know that?

FELIX: We guessed.

CHUCK: We're all frightfully good guessers. Whose go?

ZARA: Felix's. Come on, Lucy. You can guess, too.

LUCY: It's a ridiculous way to play.

    (FELIX *plays a card*. CHUCK *plays a card*. LUCY *plays a card*.)

    (*Sulkily*) Snap, then!

FELIX: Oh, no. Come on.

ZARA: No, no, no.

CHUCK: Play properly.

FELIX: That's just being silly, Lucy. Be sensible.

ZARA: She didn't mean it. It was a mistake.

LUCY: Yes, I did. I meant it. Let me see your cards.

    (LUCY, FELIX *and* CHUCK *turn over their cards. None are the same*.)

    Well, they might have been.

CHUCK: No way. Carry on, Zara.

    (ZARA *plays a card*. FELIX *plays a card*. CHUCK *plays a card*. LUCY *plays a card*. ZARA *plays a card*. FELIX *plays a card*. CHUCK *plays a card*. LUCY *plays a card*. As she does so, the other three let out a great roar*.)

FELIX, CHUCK and ZARA: (*Together*) SNAP!!!

    (*Again, the three laugh delightedly*. LUCY *gets up from the table angrily*.)

LUCY: That's it! I'm not playing any more. You're just cheating, all of you. It's not fair!

(*She throws her cards down on the table. Silence.*)

FELIX: Well, I don't think I want to sit here and put up with behaviour like that.

CHUCK: No.

ZARA: (*Unhappily*) No.

FELIX: I think I'll just get my coat from upstairs. Might go for a walk. It's a lovely morning.

CHUCK: Good idea.

ZARA: Fine.

(*They move to the stairs.* LUCY *watches them.*)

FELIX: Loser clears up, I think. Doesn't she, Lucy?

(LUCY *glares.* FELIX *and* CHUCK *go upstairs and off.* ZARA *lingers behind.*)

ZARA: Come on, Lucy. I'll help you. Lucy?

FELIX: (*Calling*) Zara!

ZARA: Yes, Felix.

FELIX: Here a second.

ZARA: Coming. (*To* LUCY) I'll be back. Start clearing up, there's a love. Don't spoil the day.

(ZARA *goes upstairs after* FELIX *and* CHUCK. LUCY *stands miserably.*)

LUCY: (*To audience*) I tidied away the cards. (*She starts to do so.*) But I was still angry. It wasn't fair, it really wasn't. I mean, fancy playing cards and cheating like that. Just because they could do things I couldn't. I was very upset indeed. Not even my brother Grisly Gary would have behaved like that. So, later on when they all came down again . . .

(FELIX, CHUCK *and* ZARA *all come down in their coats.*)

FELIX: Lucy, we thought we'd stroll along to the funfair. Do you want to come with us?

LUCY: (*Sulkily*) No, I don't.

ZARA: Oh, come on, Lucy.

LUCY: I don't want to go, thank you.

CHUCK: Lucy . . .

LUCY: You go.

FELIX: Oh well, suit yourself. Bye, then.

CHUCK: Bye, then.

50

ZARA: Bye.
(*They all go out of the front door and off.*)
LUCY: (*To audience*) I don't know why I said 'no'. I really wanted to go to the funfair. I think I just said 'no' to upset them. Only I didn't upset them at all, of course. I just upset me even more. They were gone for ages, too. And I sat around feeling very sorry for myself. And then I thought, 'Well, I'll try and do something to make up for it.' Maybe – give them a surprise when they get back – that's it. And I hunted around in the kitchen. And I found this cookery book.
(*She finds the book in question.*)
(*Reading*) QUICK AND EASY CAKE-MAKING by Elizabeth Spatula. And then I had this great idea. While they were out, I'd make them this delicious cake – just to say I was sorry for losing my temper. I'd never made a cake before – as I said, I'm not very good at cooking – but it said *easy* on the cover and *quick* – so it must be true or they wouldn't have been allowed to print it. (*She lays the book on the table.*) Now then. (*Reading*) 'Ingredients. Self-raising flour.'
(*She hunts for each ingredient in turn.*)
(*Finding a labelled tin*) Self-raising flour. Here we are.
(*Reading*) 'Margarine.' I know we've got that.
(*She finds the margarine from the fridge.*)
'Sugar.' (*Hunting*) Sugar – sugar – sugar . . .
(*She finds the sugar.*)
Right. (*Reading*) 'Mixed dried fruit.' Oh, now . . . more difficult . . .
(*She locates a withered orange, a black banana and a shrivelled lemon.*)
These look pretty dried. I'll mix these up. What else?
(*Reading*) 'Two eggs. Milk.' Well . . .
(*She hunts again.*)
(*At the fridge*) Oh yes, eggs, here we are. Great. Didn't know we had these. And milk. Right.
(*She comes across another packet.*)
Hey! Here's some prunes. They're dried fruit. I'll put those in as well. Good. So, those are the ingredients. Off we go. Now what? (*Reading*) 'Heat the oven.' Heat the oven.

(*She switches on the oven.*)

(*Checking*) Is that lit? Oh, yes. It lights itself. (*Reading*) 'Grease a cake tin.' (*Hunting*) Cake tin . . .

(*She finds an ordinary cake tin with a lid and* CAKE *written on it.*)

Cake tin . . . Now, grease . . . ? Oh, yes. I know. There's that stuff Dad used on our back gate when the hinges squeaked . . .

(*She locates a can of grease under the sink.*)

This should do. Grease the tin. I wonder why you have to do this?

(*She greases the tin on the outside.*)

I mean, all it does is make it slippery to pick up. Stupid. Perhaps it's to stop the lid squeaking. Yuk! Now I'm all greasy. What's next? (*Reading*) 'Large mixing bowl.' Yes. We've got one of those somewhere.

(*She finds the mixing bowl.*)

(*Reading*) 'Put the ingredients into a mixing bowl and beat well.' Right. Here goes.

(*She puts everything into the bowl – whole eggs, unpeeled fruit and pours the sugar, flour and milk liberally over the lot.*)

Lucy Baines, Master Cook. There! It's dead easy this cake-making (*Reading*) 'Beat well . . .'

(*She finds an electric hand-held egg-beater.*)

Yeah! Great! This'll do.

(*She activates the whisk in the bowl. A lot of flour flies about.*)

That's it. (*Reading*) 'Pour into tin.' Right.

(*She does this.*)

(*Reading*) 'Bake in oven for one hour.' That's all there is to it. Don't know why Mum makes such a fuss about cooking. Anyone can do it.

(*She puts the cake in the oven.*)

(*To audience*) All I had to do then was to sit and wait. I hoped my cake would be ready before they all came back from their walk. I wanted to surprise them. It was while I was sitting there, waiting for it to cook, that I heard the voices. I may have dozed off but I don't think I did.

(*The distant, disembodied voices of her 'real' family are heard.*)

WALT: Loooooo . . . cy!

JOY: Looooo . . . cy!

GARY: Loooo . . . cy!

LUCY: (*Startled*) What's that?

WALT: Loooo . . . cy!

LUCY: Who is that? Where are you?

JOY: Lucy! Come back to us. Come back.

LUCY: Mum? Where are you?

GARY: Come back, Lucy. We're sorry.

LUCY: Gary? I can hear you but I can't see you . . .

WALT: I'm ever so sorry, love. We didn't mean to make you unhappy . . .

LUCY: Dad? Why can't I see any of you?

(*The voices start to recede.*)

WALT: Looo . . . cy!

JOY: Loooo . . . cy!

GARY: Looooo . . . cy!

LUCY: (*Calling after them*) Mum? Dad? Gary? Come back! Come back!

(FELIX, CHUCK *and* ZARA *appear at the front door, unexpectedly.*)

FELIX: We're back.

CHUCK: It's all right.

ZARA: Don't worry.

LUCY: (*A little disappointed*) Oh.

FELIX: Well, try and look a bit pleased to see us.

LUCY: Yes. Hallo.

ZARA: The funfair was great. Wasn't it?

CHUCK: Wonderful.

FELIX: Terrific.

LUCY: Yes, I expect it was.

ZARA: Sorry you didn't come. You'd have loved it. Wouldn't she?

CHUCK: She certainly would. You should have come.

FELIX: You should have done. Pity you didn't.

LUCY: (*Muttering*) Yes. (*To audience*) I wish they wouldn't go on about it.

FELIX: And what have you been doing, Lucy? You look as if you've been busy.

LUCY: Yes, I was . . . I've made you a surprise . . .

CHUCK: A surprise!

ZARA: Wonderful! How exciting!

LUCY: Wait! I think it's ready. You have to close your eyes. All of you, close your eyes . . .

FELIX: We will.

CHUCK: All right.

ZARA: OK.

(*The three close their eyes while* LUCY *gets her cake from the oven (in a duplicate tin). She picks the tin out with a cloth, takes it to the table and tips the cake out.*)

LUCY: And lo and beho– Oh.

(*Her 'cake' is a solid uneven misshapen ball. Very heavy and solid. Dotted with prunes, a whole eggshell sticks out of one side, a lemon from the other. From the top, protrudes the black banana. The other three open their eyes.*)

Oh, dear.

FELIX: Oh.

CHUCK: Ah.

ZARA: Mm.

CHUCK: What's the point of this game? Are we supposed to try and guess what it is, is that the idea?

LUCY: No . . .

FELIX: I know, it's a piece of sculpture . . .

LUCY: No . . .

CHUCK: No, it's the head of a yeti . . .

LUCY: No . . .

ZARA: A Martian football . . . ?

LUCY: No, it's a cake . . .

FELIX: A what?

LUCY: It's meant to be a cake.

CHUCK: A cake?

ZARA: A cake. Well . . .

FELIX: Well, a cake. I'd never have guessed that in a hundred years. Well done, Lucy. Good game.

LUCY: It didn't come out like it was supposed to.

CHUCK: Never mind. Perhaps Felix will make us a cake.

ZARA: Oh, yes. Make us a cake, Dad.

FELIX: All right. I'll make a cake.

(*Under the next,* FELIX *prepares to make his cake. He finds a covered dish from a cupboard – actually one with a false lid. He lifts the lid off to reveal the empty dish. He sprinkles a little of the remaining flour on the dish with his finger and thumb, the merest drip of milk and sprinkling of sugar. The others watch him as they speak.*)

LUCY: You can't. There's nothing left to make it with. I've used up all the ingredients.

FELIX: Oh, never mind about that.

CHUCK: He doesn't need ingredients.

ZARA: He's just brilliant. He makes cakes out of thin air.

LUCY: Thin air?

ZARA: Yes.

LUCY: Cakes?

ZARA: Yes.

LUCY: (*Sceptically*) Oh yes?

ZARA: Just you watch.

LUCY: There's not going to be much of it, is there?

FELIX: Tell you what, Lucy. I'll have a bet with you. If I fail to make a delicious cake – big enough for all of us – I'll do all the cleaning up for you. That a bargain?

LUCY: Right!

FELIX: But if I do manage to make a cake, you do the clearing up. All right?

LUCY: All right.

ZARA: (*To* LUCY) Better get the broom out . . .
(FELIX *finishes his preparations. He re-covers the dish again.*)

FELIX: Right, then.

LUCY: Is that it?

FELIX: That's it.

LUCY: How long does it take to cook?

FELIX: Oh, just a second or two. And – (*He breathes on the dish.*) Just warm it up a little . . .

LUCY: (*Muttering*) Stupid.

FELIX: And – *voilà*!
(*He lifts the lid to reveal an iced cake.*)

CHUCK: (*In approval*) Yeah!

ZARA: Bravo!

FELIX: Not bad, not bad. Turned out quite well.

LUCY: (*Stunned*) How did you do that?

ZARA: I told you. He's really good at cake-making.

CHUCK: Can we have a piece now?

FELIX: Of course. Zara, fetch three plates.

ZARA: Three plates, right.

LUCY: (*Dismayed*) Three?

FELIX: None for you till you've cleaned up, Lucy. Remember our
bargain?

LUCY: (*Unhappily*) Oh. Yes.

> (*She starts to tidy up the kitchen, throwing her own cake away and
> wiping down the table.* ZARA *has found three side plates and a
> knife for the cake.*)

ZARA: Here we are.

FELIX: Splendid.

CHUCK: Yummy.

> (FELIX *cuts the cake into four.*)

FELIX: Zara . . .

ZARA: Thank you . . .

FELIX: Chuck . . .

LUCY: Save some for me . . .

FELIX: And this piece for me.

> (FELIX *takes the base with the remaining piece of cake on it,
> re-covers the dish and crosses to a cupboard.*)

> Lucy, I'm going to put your piece in the cupboard here. Now,
> I'm trusting you to keep our bargain. You mustn't eat it until
> you've finished cleaning the whole house. All right?

LUCY: The *whole* house?

FELIX: The whole house.

LUCY: What, *all* of it?

FELIX: Yes. Including the attic.

LUCY: The *attic*?

FELIX: And the cellar. It's your house, after all.

CHUCK: You'd better get going, hadn't you?

ZARA: Or your cake will get stale.

LUCY: That isn't fair at all.

FELIX: No cheating, now.

CHUCK: No cheating.

ZARA: No cheating.

(*The three sit to enjoy their cake.* LUCY *scowls and tidies a little more.*)

LUCY: I was beginning to get a bit fed up with these three. I mean, this is my house. I'll do what I like in it.

(*She crosses to the TV.*)

(*Sarcastically*) If no one has any objections, I'd like some music whilst I'm working, if you don't mind. Thank you very much.

(*She switches on the TV. The test card appears. Loud pop music.*) All right? Thank you very much.

(LUCY *returns to her kitchen-tidying.* FELIX *motions at the set with his finger and thumb. The music changes to something gently classical.* LUCY *stamps back to the set.*)

Excuse me. I preferred the music that was on before.

(*She snaps the TV set switch back on to the pop music.*)

Thank you very much.

(*She returns to her work. She has scarcely got back to work before* CHUCK *has effected another channel change back to the classical music.* ZARA *laughs.*)

(*Returning, furiously*) Will you kindly leave this television set alone?

ZARA: Nobody's touched it.

(LUCY *switches the set back to the pop music, glares at them, and makes to go back to the kitchen area. She has not gone two feet before* ZARA *has again altered the channel back to the classical music.*)

(*Screaming at them*) Look, will you all stop doing this? Will you stop it. STOP IT!

(*She seizes the TV knob altogether too roughly. It comes away in her hand. She is left holding the knob, which is attached to a long spring and a mass of loose wires. The TV makes a strange warbling sound, gurgles and dies.*)

(*Tearfully*) Now look what you've made me do. Look what you've made me do.

(*Slight pause. They stare at her.*)

FELIX: I think if you'll all excuse me, I'm going to finish my cake upstairs. It's just a bit too noisy down here.

(*He rises.*)

CHUCK: (*Rising too*) It certainly is. I'll join you.

ZARA: (*Also rising*) Yes, I will too. Lovely cake, Felix.

CHUCK: Terrific. Thank you.

(ZARA *leads the way upstairs, followed by* CHUCK *and then* FELIX. LUCY *glares at them.*)

LUCY: Well, I'm going to have my piece now, so there. I'm going to eat my piece. I don't care.

(LUCY *marches to the cupboard, opens the door, takes out the dish and sets it on the table. She lifts the lid. Her piece of cake has gone. In its place is half a brick with a candle in it.*)

What – ?

FELIX: (*As he goes*) Now, I did warn you, Lucy. I warned you.

(*He goes upstairs, laughing as he does so. The other two join in the laughter and sing a quick burst of 'Happy Birthday to You'. During the next,* ZARA *goes into Lucy's room and lies on Lucy's bed.* CHUCK *goes into Gary's room and does the same.* FELIX *goes off to Joy's and Walt's room.* LUCY *clears away the cake dish as she speaks. The kitchen by now is back to normal.*)

LUCY: (*To audience*) I was beginning to get a little bit nervous, I don't mind saying. They seemed to be taking over the house, me, everything. And there didn't seem to be much I could do to stop them.

(*Distant voices are heard, faintly and briefly.*)

JOY, WALT *and* GARY: (*In unison*) Looooo . . . cy!

LUCY: (*Calling softly*) Mum? Dad? Are you there? Gary? Can you hear me? Mum? (*She listens.*) But I must have imagined them again. They won't come back – ever. They've gone. (*Slightly tearful*) And I made them go. I was all alone. How will I ever get them back? What did Zara say? Anything's possible, if you put your mind to it. Come back, Mum! Come back Dad! Oh, it's no use. I sat downstairs for ages. I didn't really want to go upstairs. Not even to see Zara. Once she'd been my friend, my very best friend in the world – but not any more. She'd changed.

(*The lights have dimmed.*)

But as it got later and I got tireder and tireder I thought, 'No, why shouldn't I sleep in my own bed?' It was my bed. This is my house.

(*Slight pause.*)

(*Determinedly*) I'm going upstairs.

(LUCY *goes up to her room. She opens the door to find* ZARA *lying on her bed.*)

ZARA: (*Casually*) Oh, hi!

LUCY: What are you doing?

ZARA: Mmm?

LUCY: That's my bed, get off my bed. That's your bed, there.

ZARA: No, I think we take it in turns, Lucy, that's only fair.

LUCY: Get off! I want my bed.

ZARA: That's your bed, there.

LUCY: No, it isn't.

ZARA: (*Colder*) It is tonight.

LUCY: You get off my bed or I'll . . . or I'll . . .

ZARA: (*Sitting up and staring at her, dangerously*) Or you'll what?

LUCY: (*Nervously*) You'd better be careful, that's all.

ZARA: I think you're the one who has to be careful, Lucy. Very, very careful indeed.

(ZARA *smiles nastily. She looks up at Lucy's bookshelf. The books start to jump off the shelf, one by one.* LUCY *tries to save them.* ZARA *laughs.*)

LUCY: Stop it! Please, please, stop it. Stop it!

(*The books stop falling.* LUCY *gathers them up protectively.*)

ZARA: Now get into bed like a good little girl.

(LUCY *thinks about replying but doesn't. She returns the books to the shelf and lies on the folding bed.*)

LUCY: (*As she does so*) Ooh! Ow! This is a terrible bed. I'll never sleep on this.

ZARA: Ssssh! Go to sleep.

(ZARA *gestures and the lights go out in the bedroom.*)

Goodnight.

LUCY: (*To audience*) It was all very well for her to talk but I couldn't get to –

ZARA: (*Fiercely*) Shhh!

LUCY: (*In a whisper*) . . . I couldn't get to sleep at all. The bed had so many – struts and – pointed bits. It was like trying to sleep in the – bottom of a – rowing boat. Ow!

ZARA: Lucy! You are making a noise. Shut up.

LUCY: This is uncomfortable. I can't sleep on this.

ZARA: Then go and sleep somewhere else.

LUCY: Where?

ZARA: I don't know. On the floor, somewhere.

LUCY: I'm not sleeping on the floor. I want my bed back. Give me my bed.

(*The lights come on. ZARA sits up, looking menacing. She extends her arm; seemingly, LUCY is gripped by an invisible force.*)

ZARA: I'm warning you, Lucy. One more sound and I'll make sure you never sleep again. I'll glue your eyelids open for ever.

(*She releases her. LUCY swallows.*)

Goodnight.

(*The lights go out again. After a second, LUCY tosses and turns uncomfortably.*)

LUCY: Ooof! Eeee! Aaaa!

ZARA: (*Growling*) Lucy!

(*LUCY gets up off the bed.*)

LUCY: I'm sorry. I'm sorry. Don't glue my eyelids, please! All right. All right. You win. I'll go and sleep somewhere else, then. But I'm having my bed back tomorrow night, so there.

ZARA: We'll see.

LUCY: (*Snatching up her blanket*) We certainly will.

(*LUCY goes out of her bedroom, closes the door and lies down on the landing.*)

(*Muttering to herself*) I'll sleep here then. Good as anywhere else. It's my house, I don't see why I have to sleep on the landing. Why doesn't somebody else sleep on the landing? Why has it got to be me? It's not fair. It's not fair . . .

(*During this last, CHUCK has got off his bed and opens the door.*)

CHUCK: I say, do you have to lie out here making all that din?

LUCY: I wasn't making a din.

CHUCK: You were, you were making the most terrible racket. Now, if you want to do that, I'd rather you didn't lie outside my door to do it. Go and lie somewhere else, all right?

LUCY: I can lie where I like, this is my house.

(*CHUCK reaches out a hand and practically lifts LUCY off the floor with an invisible force.*)

CHUCK: Now don't get me angry, please. Just remember how good

I am at tidying things away. Be careful, or I might decide to tidy you away. Permanently. OK? (*He 'drops' her back on the floor with a thump.*)

LUCY: (*Getting up hurriedly*) Where do I sleep then?

CHUCK: What about downstairs? Go on. Get off downstairs.

(CHUCK *goes back into Gary's room and closes the door.* LUCY *goes downstairs, clutching her blanket.*)

LUCY: (*Muttering again*) Don't see why I have to go downstairs. Why do I have to sleep down here? It's not fair. It's my house. Why doesn't somebody else sleep down here, that's what I want to know.

(*She sits in the armchair and wraps the blanket round her.*)

Aah! This is even more uncomfortable than the floor. I can't sleep in this chair. Mum! Dad! Please come back. I'm sorry. Please come back. Just put your mind to it, Lucy, just put your mind to it. I won't be rotten about you ever again. I won't even be rotten to Gary. Well, maybe just a bit, but not as much. Mum! Just put my mind to it . . .

(FELIX *has appeared on the stairs.*)

FELIX: Lucy!

LUCY: (*Startled*) Who's that?

FELIX: Please try not to make quite so much noise. People are trying to sleep.

LUCY: So am I. I'm trying to sleep.

FELIX: Well, do it a little more quietly, like everyone else.

LUCY: (*Wailing, loudly*) It's all right for them, they've got beds. I haven't even got a bed. Why can't I have a bed!

ZARA: ⎫ (*From upstairs*) Be quiet!
CHUCK: ⎬(*Together*) (*From upstairs*) Shut up!
FELIX: ⎭ (*Fiercely*) LUCY!

(*Slight pause.* FELIX *reaches out his arm and seemingly grips* LUCY *by her nose.* LUCY *reacts.*)

FELIX: (*Quietly*) Lucy, you are a noisy, untidy, bad-mannered, dirty, smelly, ignorant, thoroughly unprepossessing lump of a girl.

LUCY: (*In pain*) Ow, by dose . . .

FELIX: I don't want to hear another sound from you, is that clear? Now goodnight.

(*He releases* LUCY. *She falls to the ground.* FELIX *goes off to his room.*)

LUCY: (*In a whisper*) I am not smelly. I bath – lots of times. Every other – time I can. I'm not a lump either. (*Slightly louder*) I am not a lump. I'm in the school swimming team. I couldn't swim if I was a lump, could I? (*Reflecting*) I was in the school swimming team, anyway. Mum! Oh, Mum! Just put your mind to it . . .

(*There is a soft knocking at the front door.* LUCY *stops and listens.*) What's that?

(*The knocking is repeated, softly.*)

Mum? Is that you? Mum?

(LUCY *creeps to the door, still clutching her blanket, and listens.*)

Dad? Gary? Who's out there? (*Opening the front door cautiously*) Hallo? Anybody here?

(*She ventures outside a little way, very cautiously. She looks up and down the street. Suddenly the front door closes behind her.*)

Hey!

(*She tries the door but it is locked.*)

Oh, no. Now I'm locked out. (*Knocking on the door*) Somebody. I say. Hallo! Hallo!

(*Down the street a dog barks. Then a baby starts crying.*)

Oh! It's freezing out here. (*Shouting*) Help! Help!

(*From up the street an angry voice shouts: 'Be quiet down there!'*)

(*Indignantly*) Be quiet yourself. I'm locked out! Oh.

(*She puts her mouth to the letter box.*)

(*Shouting through it*) Hallo! Hallo! (*Giving up*) Oh, this is hopeless. I must get someone to hear me or I'll freeze to death. Zara! I'll see if I can wake her up. If I throw some small stones at the window, she might hear.

(*She gathers a handful of gravel and throws it at the window. Sounds as it hits the window.* ZARA *sits up in bed.*)

(*Calling softly, as she throws more gravel*) Zara! Zara!

(ZARA *comes to the window and looks out.*)

ZARA: (*Crossly*) What is it? What do you want?

LUCY: Help me. Can you help me?

ZARA: Why?

LUCY: I'm locked out. Can't you see, I'm locked out?

62

ZARA: Yes, I know you are.

LUCY: You knew? Then why didn't you – ?

ZARA: Because I locked you out, Lucy.

LUCY: (*Hurt*) Why? Why did you do that?

ZARA: Because we don't want you here any more. We don't want you living with us.

LUCY: Why not? Zara! You used to be my friend. My best friend. My invisible friend. Why are you doing this? What have I ever done to you?

ZARA: Felix told you, Lucy. He's already told you. You are noisy. You are untidy. You don't know how to behave properly. You're just not someone that nice people want to live with, that's all. Goodnight. (*She makes to go inside again.*)

LUCY: Zara!

ZARA: What?

LUCY: Do you think I'm smelly as well?

ZARA: Oh yes. Most definitely. Very, very smelly. Goodbye.
(ZARA *withdraws her head through the window. The house is in darkness. Lights only on* LUCY *in the road. During the next, both* ZARA *and* CHUCK *go off unseen.*)

LUCY: (*Wailing*) What am I going to do now? I can't stay out here all night. Where am I going to go?
(*A car passes.* LUCY *waves into the headlights but it speeds on past and into the night.*)
(*As it passes*) Hey! Hey! I say. (*Dejected*) Oh. (*A sudden thought*) I know. There might be a window open somewhere. If I could climb in without them hearing me . . . I could get a few things together. My money's all in my desk. Yes, that's it. Get some money. I need money. Then maybe I can catch an all-night bus – or even a taxi to Auntie Gertie's. I can't stand Auntie Gertie, her and her big fat budgie, but anything's better than freezing to death out here. (*Looking up at the house*) Yes, I think I could, climb up there without them hearing me. It's worth a try. Here goes. Wish me luck. (*To audience*) Ssshhh!
(*A sequence where* LUCY *climbs up to an upstairs window. The more tension and thrills the better. At one point at least, she nearly falls. Finally she reaches her bedroom, either via that window or another first-floor window.*)

63

(*Looking round the room*) Zara's not here. Odd. Now, quickly. Money.

(*She rummages in her desk drawer.*)

Where is it? I wish I could turn the light on, but I daren't risk it. Have to be so quiet too. Chuck's next door and he hears everything. Ah, here we are. My whole fortune. Seven pounds fifty-two p. Terrific. Go to Hong Kong for that. If I walked. Right. (*Looking at the window*) Not going back that way. I'll risk the stairs.

(*She tiptoes out of her room and along the landing. She starts to descend the stairs.*)

(*Whispering*) Shh! Quietly! One of these creaks. I can never remember which one.

(*Loud creak as she treads on a stair.*)

Whoops! That's the one. Nearly there . . . Nearly there!

(*Suddenly,* ZARA *appears at the bottom of the stairs.*)

ZARA: Gotcha!

LUCY: (*Startled*) Ah!

ZARA: What are you doing in our house?

LUCY: Me?

ZARA: What are you doing here?

LUCY: This isn't your house.

ZARA: Oh, yes, it is.

LUCY: This is my house.

ZARA: Not any more it isn't. You're trespassing. You're breaking and entering. You should be locked up and put in prison . . .

LUCY: Nonsense.

ZARA: You've even stolen money from us, haven't you?

LUCY: I have not.

ZARA: Seven pounds fifty-two pence. Don't lie, I even know how much was there . . .

LUCY: So do I. I knew how much was there, too. It's my money.

ZARA: Prove it, then.

LUCY: I don't have to prove it.

ZARA: Tell me the number of the note. Do you know the number on that five-pound note?

LUCY: No, of course I don't.

ZARA: Ah, but I do you see. RE59 778752. Did you know that?

LUCY: No.

ZARA: There you are then. That proves it must be mine.

LUCY: How do you know that's the number?

ZARA: Because I'm a very good guesser, that's why. (*Starting to advance on her*) Thief! You'll go to prison for years, you will. Do you know the date on the fifty-pence piece, then?

LUCY: (*Retreating from her up the stairs*) No.

ZARA: Thief! What's the date, thief?

LUCY: (*Desperately*) I don't know! I don't know!

(CHUCK *appears at the top of the stairs.* FELIX *also appears.*)

CHUCK: Nineteen eighty.

LUCY: (*Jumping, as she sees them*) Wah!

ZARA: She didn't know that.

FELIX: Because she's a thief.

CHUCK: Thief!

ZARA: Thief!

FELIX: What about the two-p piece? Going to tell us the date of that, are you?

LUCY: I don't know. (*Desperately trying to look at the coins in her hand*) I can't see it, it's too dark.

FELIX: Come on, it's easy.

ZARA: Easy!

FELIX: Easy!

LUCY: I don't know.

FELIX, CHUCK *and* ZARA: (*Together*) Nineteen eighty-three! Thief!

(FELIX *and* CHUCK *begin to advance upon* LUCY *during the next. Also, under the next, the voices of* WALT, JOY *and* GARY *are heard, as before disembodied and distant but steadily increasing in volume.*)

WALT, JOY *and* GARY: (*Together, a repeated cry*) Lucy! Lucy!

FELIX: Thief!

CHUCK: Thief!

ZARA: Thief!

LUCY: I'm not . . .

FELIX *and* CHUCK: (*Together*) Thief! Thief!

LUCY: Stop it!

FELIX, CHUCK *and* ZARA: (*Together*) Thief! Thief! Thief!

(*With a great cry, over the increasing hubbub*) STOP IT! STOP
IT! STOP IT! ZARA . . . !
(LUCY, *intent on retreating from* FELIX *and* CHUCK, *loses her
footing on the stairs and topples down them, mirroring the fall she
had earlier in the play. She lands at* ZARA'*s feet. A quick blackout.*
FELIX'*s,* CHUCK'*s and* ZARA'*s chant stops but the other from the
real family continues.* FELIX *and* CHUCK *exit in the blackout.*
JOY, WALT *and* GARY *enter and gather with* ZARA *around* LUCY.
The calls of 'Lucy' are now taken up live. ZARA *is also calling her
name gently. The lights come up on an anxious group, waiting for*
LUCY *to regain consciousness.* ZARA *has changed her appearance
just fractionally. Maybe a pair of glasses. She is adjusting the
blanket around* LUCY. *Later, we will see that the whole house is
back as it was before* LUCY'*s first fall. Gary's bedroom, for
instance, has 'untidied' itself again.*)

ZARA: (*Gently*) Lucy! Lucy! Come on. Lucy!

JOY: Lucy!

WALT: Lucy!

GARY: Lucy!

(LUCY *groans.*)

ZARA: It's all right. She's coming round.

JOY: Is she going to be all right, Doctor?

ZARA: She may have a slight concussion. But I'm sure she'll be fine.
Nothing seems to be broken anyway.

JOY: Oh, thank God. Thank God.

LUCY: (*Drowsily*) Mum! Mum!

JOY: I'm here, love, I'm here.

LUCY: (*Relieved*) Mum?

JOY: It's all right, love. Talk to her, Dad, talk to her.

WALT: Hallo then, Lucy. It's your dad here speaking, Lucy.

LUCY: Dad!

JOY: That's your dad speaking, Lucy. And here's Gary. You
remember Gary.

GARY: Hallo, Lucy.

LUCY: Oh, hallo, Grisly. (*She tries to sit up.*) If you put your mind to
it, you can . . . You can . . .

ZARA: No, don't sit up. Just lie still.

LUCY: (*Seeing her for the first time*) Who are . . . ? Who are . . . ?

66

Zara? What are you doing here? Zara?

ZARA: That's the name she was saying before.

LUCY: Zara?

ZARA: (*To* JOY) Who's Zara, do you know? Is it a friend of hers?

JOY: Oh. That'll be her invisible friend, Doctor.

WALT: Like imaginary, in her head, you know.

ZARA: Oh, yes. I understand. A lot of children have those.

WALT: Do they?

JOY: Fancy.

LUCY: Zara?

JOY: I think she thinks you're Zara, Doctor.

ZARA: Yes. Possibly.

JOY: This is Doctor Ziegler, love. From down the road. Your dad went out and telephoned her. You were lying so still, we thought you were dead.

LUCY: You're not Zara.

ZARA: No. I'm a doctor, Lucy. You've had a bit of a fall. You're going to feel a bit bruised and dizzy for a while but you're going to be fine. The ambulance is here. The men are just fetching a stretcher for you. Just try and lie still till it comes.

LUCY: (*Alarmed*) Ambulance?

ZARA: I want you to go into hospital overnight, Lucy. Just so they can keep a proper eye on you.

LUCY: I don't want to leave here. I can't leave here.

ZARA: Just overnight.

LUCY: I'll get locked out. They'll lock me out again if I go.

WALT: We're not going to lock you out, love. This is your home. We won't lock her out, will we?

GARY: No, we wouldn't lock her out. Probably.

JOY: Gary! (*To* ZARA) Does she have to go in, Doctor? I mean, we could keep an eye on her. Couldn't we?

WALT: Oh yes.

GARY: Yes.

ZARA: Well, I can't force her to go to hospital, but I really would prefer it.

JOY: I thought we'd lost her, you see. I really thought we'd lost her. I mean, if I thought we'd lost her – well, I don't know what I'd have done if I thought we'd lost her . . . (*Grasping* LUCY

67

emotionally) Oh, my baby. Oh, my baby.

LUCY: Ouch! Mum, steady on!

ZARA: Careful!

WALT: Careful, Joy.

GARY: Careful, Mum.

JOY: (*Weeping now*) Oh, we're so glad you're back with us, love. We're so grateful you were spared. We'll take care of you. I promise you we'll take special care of you.

LUCY: (*To audience*) She's a very emotional woman my mother, once she gets going. (*To* JOY) Thanks, Mum. I'm in the school swimming team. Did I tell you?

JOY: Oh, that's wonderful. Did you hear that, Walt? She's in the school swimming team. Isn't that wonderful?

WALT: Oh, that's wonderful, love. Did you hear that, Gary? She's in the school swimming team. Isn't that wonderful?

GARY: Wonderful. Dog-paddle team, is it?

JOY: You shut up. Or I'll burn your headphones.

(*The 'ambulance men' arrive at the front door, with the stretcher. They are, of course,* FELIX *and* CHUCK, *now in uniform.*)

FELIX: (*Cheerfully*) Here we are, back again. How is she then?

ZARA: She's regained consciousness. She seems all right.

CHUCK: (*To* LUCY, *gently*) Now, love. We're just going lift you on to this, all right. Don't try and do it yourself, just relax . . .

LUCY: (*Recognizing him*) Chuck?

FELIX: Chuck? No, we won't chuck you, love, I promise. We'll just lift you.

LUCY: Felix!

CHUCK: Come on, then. Upsidaisy.

LUCY: No, get away. Mum! Don't let them touch me! Don't let them touch me!

(CHUCK *and* FELIX *back off, startled at her vehemence.*)

FELIX: It's all right. It's all right. We're not going to hurt you.

JOY: It's all right, Lucy.

WALT: It's all right.

CHUCK: (*Aside, to* ZARA) Concussion, is it?

ZARA: (*Softly, to* CHUCK) She's obviously had quite an emotional

68

shock. Maybe it's better if we don't try to move her. Not immediately. She may be better if she stays here in familiar surroundings.

FELIX: Come on. We're only going to lift you on to this, that's all.

LUCY: Get away, Felix, get away from me.

JOY: Lucy! It's only the ambulance man . . .

FELIX: My name's George, love. And him there's Harry. (*To the others*) Felix. She thinks I'm a cat.

CHUCK: Doctor thinks maybe we should leave her, George.

FELIX: Leave her?

ZARA: Might be better. On second thoughts.

FELIX: Right, you're the doctor.

(*He starts to fold up the stretcher again.*)

ZARA: Sorry to have called you out.

CHUCK: That's all right. All in a night's work. (*Mock sternly to* LUCY) Just you go carefully on those stairs in future. All right? Worried everyone to death, you have.

LUCY: (*Meekly*) Sorry.

FELIX: Goodnight, all.

CHUCK: Goodnight, all.

ALL: Goodnight.

(FELIX *and* CHUCK *leave.*)

ZARA: Now, are you strong enough to sit up, Lucy?

LUCY: Yes, I think so.

JOY: Carefully, love.

WALT: Careful.

GARY: Carefully.

ZARA: That's it. Now I want you to take your weight on me and try and walk as far as that chair. Are you ready?

LUCY: Yes.

ZARA: And one, two, three – up . . .

(LUCY *lifts herself to her feet with* ZARA's *help. Once up, she sways uncertainly.*)

LUCY: Ah!

ZARA: Help her someone!

(*They all rush forward together, nearly knocking* LUCY *over again in their eagerness to help.*)

JOY: Here!

WALT: Here!

GARY: Here!

ZARA: Carefully, now. Just one of you will do.

JOY: Sorry.

WALT: Sorry.

GARY: Sorry.

> (*They all step back again. Somehow* ZARA *gets* LUCY *to the chair unaided, where she sits her down.*)

ZARA: There! Well done, Lucy. Clever girl. (*Turning*) Now. For the next day or so, she is not to be left alone. Not for a single minute. Is that understood?

JOY: Yes.

WALT: Yes, Doctor.

GARY: Yes.

ZARA: (*Sternly*) I shall pop round to see her regularly but in between times I don't want her moving unnecessarily for any reason at all. She must have complete rest. Complete quiet. First sign of any stress or over-exertion and she goes straight into hospital, no arguments. Understood?

JOY: Yes, Doctor.

WALT: Yes.

GARY: Yes, Doctor.

ZARA: (*Scrawling on her pad*) First thing in the morning, you get these from a chemist. They're to be taken four-hourly over twenty-four hours. Understood?

JOY: Yes.

WALT: Yes, Doctor.

GARY: Yes.

ZARA: Good. Goodnight, Lucy. Try and get some sleep.

LUCY: Can I have my bed back?

ZARA: Yes, of course you can have your bed.

LUCY: Thank you.

ZARA: I'll look in again in the morning.

JOY: Thank you, Doctor.

WALT: Thank you.

GARY: Thank you, Doctor.

ZARA: (*As she goes*) Goodnight.

JOY: Goodnight.

WALT: Goodnight, Doctor.

GARY: Goodnight.

(ZARA *goes out through the front door.*)

JOY: Right. Now what can we get you love? You just say the word. We're all here to look after you. Aren't we?

WALT: Yes.

GARY: Oh, yes.

JOY: What can we get you, love?

LUCY: I'm a little bit cold.

JOY: Cold, she's cold. Gary!

GARY: Yes, Mum.

JOY: Fetch your sister another blanket. Quickly.

GARY: Yes, Mum.

JOY: And a pillow. Fetch her a pillow. Quickly.

GARY: Yes, Mum.

(GARY *sprints upstairs.*)

JOY: Walter. Put the kettle on, make her a hot-water bottle. Quickly.

WALT: Right.

(WALT *goes to do this.*)

JOY: I'll make you some hot chocolate. Would you like that?

LUCY: Lovely. Thank you, Mum.

(JOY *goes to do this.*)

(*To audience*) The next few days were great. They were all running all over the place for me. Nothing was too much trouble. I lived like a princess. Mum brought me hot meals in bed every two hours. Gary stopped playing his music. And Dad only had the TV programmes on that I wanted to watch. More important still, they all started actually *talking* to me. It was amazing. A miracle.

(*Simultaneously,* GARY *arrives with a second blanket and a pillow from upstairs.* WALT *arrives with a hot-water bottle,* JOY *brings her a mug of chocolate. They all fuss around her, arranging pillows and tucking in rugs, etc. They all move away from her again under the next, leaving* LUCY *alone.*)

Of course, it couldn't last for ever. But it was great while it did. I mean, I'd love to be able to tell you that after that we were all tremendously happy for ever like the end of some romantic movie – you know . . .

(*A burst of romantic music. Pretty lights.*)

WALT: (*To* JOY, *with great emotion*) Darling. Oh, my darling.

JOY: Oh, my darling darling . . .

WALT: Oh, darling . . .

GARY: Hallo, darlings . . .

WALT *and* JOY: (*Together*) Darling!

(*They all embrace each other.*)

LUCY: Hallo, darlings. It's me.

ALL: Darling!

(*The music stops, the lights revert. Everyone resumes their former positions. The family exit, under the next.*)

LUCY: But it wasn't like that. Then things never are, not in real life. But I think we'd all learned something. We did try to get on with each other a bit more. Mum, Dad and Gary – they each made an effort, in their own way. (*She gets up from the chair.*) As for me – well, I made an effort, too. And I steered well clear of any more invisible friends, I can tell you. Enough of that. Still, all in all, life's a great improvement. So if there's anything to be learnt from what occurred, it's this: if you put your mind to it – you can make practically anything happen for you. Anything. Like this.

(*She points to the vase, back on the table.*)

Everybody – concentrate and when I tell you, think of the word 'move' very hard. Are you ready? After three then. One . . . two . . . three . . . and MOVE . . .

(*The vase fails to move.*)

No? Try again. Think harder this time. And . . . one . . . two . . . three . . . and MOVE . . .

(*Still nothing happens.*)

No. We can't be thinking hard enough. One last time. We can do it. One . . . two . . . three . . . and MOVE!

(*This time the vase moves all along the table.*)

(*Triumphantly*) YES!!! Didn't I tell you? Anything's possible! Anything! Bye.

(*She waves to the audience and goes off.*)

(*Blackout*)